THE EVERGREEN EXECUTIVE

how to keep going and keep growing as a leader

Sandra Webber

RETHINK PRESS

First published in Great Britain in 2020 by
Rethink Press (www.rethinkpress.com)

© Copyright Sandra Webber

Praise

'Sandra has a clarity and purposefulness in her words that really resonate with me as an ambitious, development-focused leader. Having had the wonderful opportunity to be coached by Sandra and hearing that same support and challenge leap from the page here, I can honestly say this book will be more than worth your time and will fast become a trusted guide you can refer back to again and again. Thank you, Sandra!'

—Richard Orna, Head of Information Services, energy supplier

'A thought-provoking book that made me reflect on how I am performing as a leader and what I need to do to continue to develop. I wish it had been written at the start of my leadership journey. It is a fabulous toolkit that I will refer to time and time again, and I can't wait to share it with the teams that I lead and support.'

—Claire Davis, L&D director, accountancy firm

'Thanks for another great and immersive read Sandra. Once again, it was easy to put "myself" into the book thanks to how you have written it; I find the exercises in each chapter really help with that. So much resonates with me and the people around me – good, bad and otherwise! Time for some honesty and self-assessment now, before thinking about my action plan.'

—Becky Forster, pensions software trainer

'This has been a fantastic book to read at the start of my leadership career. There is good advice on how to think about your own behaviour and how to improve. Working with the method is going to help me improve myself and my career.'

—**Dave Shepherd,** senior design/development engineer

'This is an excellent book, with great, proven methods for becoming a better leader in any working environment. It has well-thought-out and practical applications. Sandra's wealth of experience, knowledge and understanding really shine through. It is packed with simple steps to start making a difference, to help you on your journey to become more professional and for continuing development.'

—**Martyn Hinam,** leisure centre manager
and tai chi instructor

'A masterpiece full of practical takeaways and inspiring motivation. The only reason you'll want to put this book down is so that you can go off and implement some of the great strategies and theories so brilliantly articulated within. Perfect.'

—**Neil Trevena,** performance specialist,
water company

'Great book. It's full of really clear, practical tools and strategies that I know work because I successfully employed them when I was coached by Sandra. I would encourage managers to read this book and use these tools if they want to improve performance.'

—**Angela Spreadbury,** Director of Finance and
Resources, SS Great Britain Trust

To all those leaders I have worked with who have inspired me, and to all the Rays of Sunshine who have supported me, both professionally and personally.

Contents

Foreword

If you have ever done any serious trekking or mountain climbing, you will be familiar with sherpas. To me these rugged, highly skilled and trustworthy guides epitomise the highest and most effective type of leadership. Why? Because they represent the three qualities I have found vital to success as a leader. First, these are individuals with such unassailable and tested competence that the climbers they lead are willing to place their complete and total trust in them. Second, they have the ability to get you to the summit (or at least, in my experience, to base camp!) without incident – if you are willing to focus on their plans (maps) and strategies. And third, their responsibility is to protect, encourage and inspire those who are dependent on them to win. Their own lives and the lives of their climbers are totally bound together in a life-preserving mission.

I find it fascinating that today the study of leadership and the training for it has proliferated in schools and universities – even starting at the primary level – in blogs, webinars and speeches, and in a bursting library of published books about the subject. Those who are considered effective leaders are profiled in business magazines and columns are written about them. The individuals who are believed to have extraordinary leadership abilities are extolled as icons in various fields and then sent out on lucrative public speaking tours. And yet, with all this focus on the subject of leadership, high levels of achievement in leadership practices nevertheless often allude us. Too often, we are left with and even suffer from records of failed leadership. The human and economic cost of poor to merely acceptable leadership in organisations is significant. The remedy, I think, may be found in a deeper understanding of the things that arrest, interfere with or draw an individual away from exhibiting the qualities of true and effective leadership. After all, from my experience in corporate management, it takes courage and self-sacrifice to meet the highest standards of leadership. At a minimum, we need to find out why we sometimes lack the kinds of leaders that we deserve and the world needs.

Not shrinking from this challenge, my friend and former colleague from our days at Hewlett Packard,

Sandra Webber, has accepted the challenge and has given us a tour de force on the subject. Having observed and worked with Sandra, I know she is a person of tireless energy and dogged determination to address any issue head on and then devise the solution. She may have done just this with her new book, *The Evergreen Executive.* In reading it, you get the feeling that Sandra has poured out her whole heart and soul, as she shares, intimately with the reader, the trials and tribulations she herself has gone through as a business executive. This is the Sandra I know and respect. Now she is sharing herself with her readers, and I suspect there will be many.

What the reader will find unique about this book on leadership is that it is a complete guide and handbook written by a coach who confronts the challenges of students who would become better leaders themselves. She has thought of everything – every aspect of leadership, from adequate sleep to winning strategies. If you take it slowly, answer all the questions within, take the tests she recommends and explore the extra reading she assigns, you will have completed the equivalent of a college degree in leadership. What's more, the case studies and examples drawn from her own life make the book eminently readable and the information more practical and accessible to the reader/student.

Another aspect of the book I admire and agree with is Sandra's holistic definition of a leader. Clearly, to her, a leader or effective executive is one who is well rounded, balanced, smart, energetic, strategic, and yet sensitive to the needs of others and available to the people under their guidance and responsibility. I know I would like to achieve and live by the lofty and yet practical aspects of leadership the way she has articulated them. If any discerning executive striving to do better by their organisation absorbs and practises even a percentage of what Sandra has set out here, our companies and our world will be a better place.

She has set a high standard and renewed in me a desire to do a better job in my role. She may just be the sherpa that the world of management needs right now.

Mark Hawkins

President and Chief Financial Officer,
Salesforce, Inc.

Introduction

'Leadership and learning are indispensable to each other.'

JOHN F KENNEDY

You're in a leadership position and it's tougher than you thought. Either you're new to it or you think that it should be easier than this and you're missing a few tricks. Are you working in a chaotic business or with a dysfunctional team and doubting your skills as a leader? Maybe you're a seasoned leader but feel you're losing your spark and lacking the enthusiasm you once had in the earlier years of your career. Maybe factors outside work are causing you concern. Whatever the reason, you don't feel 100% happy with your performance as a leader and/or how you're juggling your professional and personal life.

Do you feel like you're suffering from burnout or imposter syndrome? These terms are widespread, and I hear them a lot in my work. If you've ever suffered from either, you know they're not nice places to be and require corrective action on your part. Let's look at each in turn.

Feeling burnt out is similar to feeling stressed out, and it often manifests in the physical, mental or social side of life. When you're burnt out, you're prone to getting sick, you're tired, you're irritable and you generally lack energy 24/7, even for things you used to enjoy. For whatever reason, you're struggling to cope with the demands put on you. If you don't catch burnout in its early stages, you can end up with more complicated health issues that could result in your signing off work for long periods of time. The body has a tendency to stop you in your tracks if you don't listen to it and make things impossible to continue.

Unlike burnout, which is both physical and mental, imposter syndrome is more mental – you don't feel as though you should be in your leadership role. You feel as if it's a fluke that you got it, you feel that you don't have all the skills required to do the job well and you think that eventually someone is going to find out. In meetings or other situations, you live in fear of being found out. You may be tentative in making decisions, while certain stronger personalities or those who prefer a quiet life – team members or peers – may be taking advantage, leading you not to delegate or push back as much as you could be. You may feel this way if your role came about almost by accident, with you having little prior experience or training. This can happen in a start-up situation where a good idea turns into a serious business that involves many people and needs systemising, and where leadership roles appear organically. A similar situation can occur in family-run businesses, where you, as a member of the family, find yourself in a leadership position and making things up as you go along. Lastly, you can feel like an imposter in a leadership role if you're younger than most of the people in your team.

Are you leading people who used to be your team-mates, or are there any strong personalities in your team or the wider organisation with whom you're struggling to work?

Is your career stuck or stalled? Do you feel frustrated that other colleagues seem to be leapfrogging you or are asked to get involved in more exciting work projects or initiatives? This often happens if you've been working in the same company for a long time, whether it's a large multinational or a smaller entrepreneurial organisation. You see new people being hired for positions you feel you should be in or you feel you're falling behind and haven't got the skills and knowledge that the new world needs. These feelings are stopping you from enjoying your role as much as you used to, and it's becoming harder to get by each day.

Is your work-life balance suffering? Is life outside work paying the price for the problems you have in your role? Perhaps you're working long hours, from early morning to late at night. Maybe you're constantly checking emails and working in the evenings and on weekends and family members are becoming resentful that you're never present with them physically and mentally. Maybe you no longer have the time or energy for things you used to enjoy or to be a good parent, wife, husband, partner, son, daughter, sister, brother, friend or grandparent. Whatever the issues, deep down you know your professional and personal lives aren't evenly balanced. This makes you feel uncomfortable, even if no one else has expressed their concerns.

Is your performance as a leader being questioned? Learning that your manager has concerns about your performance – during a regular one-to-one discussion or as part of the annual appraisal process – is stressful. Perhaps your manager has mentioned an aspect of your role that you acknowledge you need to do better at, or perhaps this knowledge came as a complete surprise because you thought you'd been performing well. Regardless, now that the subject has been raised, you know you need to improve your performance quickly.

This book is the result of my personal experiences of being led by various types of people, being surrounded by different leaders, and working with many people across a multitude of organisations as an executive and career coach. Some leaders have been poor, others good and some excellent. This book is based on the latter category and illustrates what I believe are the components of excellent leadership.

I learned an incredible number of leadership skills during the seventeen years I worked for US multinational technology company Hewlett Packard Ltd. I now know that their training for leaders was advanced. From the moment you either expressed an interest in a leadership role or someone suggested that you would be suitable, training would begin – with an introduction to leadership course – even before you had your first team. I also benefited due to my journey from the bottom. First, I was a temporary admin assistant; next, I acquired the permanent role of accounts payable clerk, qualified as an accountant; and then I obtained my first leadership role, followed by many senior roles. I've had the benefit of viewing the leadership role from many different levels and disciplines across a business with various challenges at each stage. I remotely managed people in different time zones, led virtual process improvement projects for short-term issues and learned the rigorous Japanese concept of total quality control. And I put all these skills into the toolkit I created a long time ago and still use today. They are the cornerstones of this book.

Over the past twenty years, I've enjoyed coaching and training leaders at all levels in a diverse range of industries. The size of the organisation or the team that you're leading doesn't matter. The basics are the same and the issues that leaders face today are similar to those they faced many years ago.

I see certain qualities again and again in leaders who keep going, keep growing and keep enjoying their work, and these are what I want to share with you in the hope they can help you wherever you're working and whatever your current challenge is.

You can keep going whatever your age, experience and activities/responsibilities outside of work. You can keep growing professionally and personally whatever stage you're at in your career. You can enjoy leadership despite the challenges that may come your way. And you can work in a smart way to make things as easy as possible – when you repeat this approach, you'll see great results.

This book will give you the framework and tools to create your own leadership footprint. It will allow you to enjoy your work and gain satisfaction in adding value to the organisations and individuals you work with.

How to use this book

My hope is that this book will be a practical one that you refer to frequently, until the habits, tools and techniques become embedded in your leadership style. You can also use it when mentoring younger leaders, to share your expertise and methods.

Feel free to adapt any of the suggested methods or templates to suit your preferred way of working. The aim is that you discover a methodology that helps you operate as a high-performing leader and, most importantly, enjoy doing so!

CHAPTER 1

What Is An Evergreen Executive?

What do I mean by the term 'Evergreen Executive'? Once you've finished this chapter, you'll have a better understanding of this type of leader and why they stand head and shoulders above the others. I also hope that when you see the contrast between the Evergreen Model of Leadership and the other three options, you'll be inspired to strive towards this. Indeed, if you're nearly there, I hope that it will help you continue the hard work it takes to maintain this over the long term. The good thing is that the more you lead in this way, the easier it gets, and the more choices you'll have in both your personal and your professional life. Consider the diagram below to start building a picture of the different types of leaders in organisations worldwide.

Leadership: The four quadrants

An Evergreen Executive operates with high levels of both personal energy and professional excellence. They pay attention to these seven areas in equal measure:

1. Physical energy

2. Mental energy

3. Relationship energy

4. Strategy

5. Stakeholders

6. Ways of working (systems)

7. Personal presence (status)

Before we explore the Evergreen Executive in more detail, let's look at the other three leadership quadrants and consider the differences.

Danger Zone (low energy/low excellence)

As the name suggests, this is a dangerous place to be. Due to the low-excellence element of this position, it's likely that some areas of the role aren't being performed to the level that they should be. Maybe deadlines are being missed, critical tasks or projects are incomplete, stakeholders are complaining that they aren't getting what's needed or you're difficult to work with, and your team may be demotivated and underperforming. If you're in this zone, you're probably aware that you are. You may have had a poor appraisal or a discussion about whether you're suitable for the role. This will be a worry that's likely to impact your personal life and relationships, leading to distress, vulnerability and ill health.

You may have been in this place before and questioning your abilities. Or it may be your first time here and you're worried that you aren't capable of fulfilling your role knowing that you may be asked to move to another role. All in all, it's an unsatisfactory position to be in, both for the individual and the organisation. If you're reading this and are worried that this sums up your position, it's possible to get out of this zone – you need good support and the right attitude when it comes to learning new ways of working. What you need is the commitment to work on the personal energy element and to strive to achieve professional excellence within your role.

Over the years, I've been asked to work with people who have just entered this quadrant. As part of their organisation's commitment to helping them, I've worked with them on their development as an external party. The key here is that the person involved needs to want to do this work. Do you want it enough?

At Risk (high energy/low excellence)

This is a challenging area for an organisation to manage because if an individual is working in this quadrant, they're normally popular and good at the interpersonal relationship side of their job thanks to their high personal energy. These people are regularly found in the canteen or around the drinks area chatting to other employees. They add energy to meetings, are fun to be around and seem to have a lot of time to spend with other people.

After a while, though, other people begin to look more closely at what these people are achieving and see that it's difficult to quantify the results they're generating. At times of reorganisation or cost cutting, these are the people who are discussed in terms of what they do, their roles within a team or the roles of their team members. When you're the subject of such discussions, your value or capability is being questioned. During cost control or downsizing, this isn't a good place to be.

People in this quadrant could be unaware of this risk. Perhaps they've been with the organisation for a long time or feel that the interpersonal energy that they bring to any role is enough to get by. Some people may be aware that their results aren't as good as they could be but aren't sure what to do about it, so they spend time building more relationships, helping others or listening to other people's problems.

Bruce

While working with a client many years ago, I kept hearing the name of one leader, Bruce,[1] who fell into this category. I wasn't coaching Bruce, but when our paths crossed due to some projects I was working on, he came across as an extremely sociable, high-energy team leader. He'd been with the organisation for a long time. In fact, people remarked that he'd been there 'forever.' I enjoyed our meetings, but he rarely seemed to take any action or lead our discussions. Those in his team said that he was a fun guy but that they weren't sure what he did and that they didn't have any one-to-one meetings with him as he felt that the team were getting on well and didn't believe such meetings were necessary.

I began to worry for Bruce when his name started coming up often during talks on organisational restructuring – senior managers were considering creating a bigger online presence over the next two years. They doubted whether Bruce

---

1   All case studies have been anonymised and some details changed to protect the confidentiality of clients.

could adapt and learn the new systems as he was beginning to resist the changes they wanted to implement and had recently joked about the company's moving towards a model where each department would be accountable for their own set of key performance indicators. He believed that this would be a fad that wouldn't last long.

Unfortunately, it wasn't long before a list of people at risk was communicated as part of the restructuring. Bruce was on the list.

I recently had an enquiry from someone who was unexpectedly put on gardening leave. At forty-three, they had to start job hunting with no CV and no idea where to begin. Sometimes situations like these – where, due to organisational changes, economic pressure or external factors, our services are no longer required by a company – can feel out of our control, but they're not if we have professional excellence that can be utilised elsewhere. High performers know that they're marketable within and outside of their current organisation and work hard to ensure that this is always the case. If they suddenly find themselves on the job market, through no fault of their own, they're well equipped to find their next role quickly.

Results at Cost (low energy/high excellence)

Many executives find themselves in this quadrant, especially if they're under pressure from their leaders or the organisation is going through challenging times (or, conversely, experiencing growth). People in this quadrant are hard workers. They want to achieve the best and be seen as people who deliver results. They often have all the data at hand, so they know where revenue is coming from or where costs are being incurred. Unfortunately, they're often so focused on the tasks and numbers that they forget to look after the people they work with and neglect their own well-being. Their energy levels, although categorised as low in this model, often peak and trough. Eventually, they reach a low point due to burnout, exhaustion or inconsistency. They may be susceptible to illnesses or even a major physical breakdown.

Those who report to these leaders often complain that they don't see them often or never get any meaningful one-to-one time or team meetings. They see their leader working crazy hours and feel guilty when they go home, thinking that they're expected to work just as long. Sometimes, these leaders can be unapproachable because they seem interested only in data and numbers, not the personal issues that a team member might want to raise.

This can be a hard quadrant for an individual to be in if they're the leader. As well as working long hours, they may be under pressure outside work. They're working to ensure that everything gets done, but when things get this bad, the leader is often under pressure at home to find another job that doesn't impact home life as much. The problem here is that if the individual hasn't mastered some of the basics, which we'll cover later in the book, their leadership pattern will repeat itself in their next role and things at home won't improve, regardless of the role.

In this quadrant, the leader becomes detached from their team members and risks personal burnout. They focus on achieving results largely by themselves rather than developing the capacity to share the load within a team. They may risk losing team members who feel disconnected and demotivated by the lack of day-to-day leadership.

PENNY

Penny fell into this category and came to see me when she realised that she needed to change her professional life and personal life but didn't know where to start.

Recently she'd had to take time off work due to ill health, something she'd never done before. She was shocked when, during a routine doctor's appointment, her blood pressure was so high that her doctor suggested she take two weeks off work to rest. Penny had had one virus after another all winter and was hoping for a course of antibiotics as exhaustion was making work difficult. With two school-aged children and a husband who travelled for work, she also had a demanding personal life.

At work she was thought of highly, always got results in her role as sales director, and more recently, with a new CEO as her manager, she'd been eager to smash her monthly sales figures to make a good impression. She'd always been ambitious, and her goal was to become CEO in a few years' time. But even though Penny had delivered great results in terms of the revenue her team was bringing in, during her annual appraisal, the new CEO expressed concern over the high staff turnover in her team.

A few people who'd recently left said during their exit interviews that they'd become demotivated because they never had any meaningful contact with Penny. The little contact they did have was centred around numbers on a spreadsheet and what they were going to do to ensure sales. Penny never asked them how they were getting on, never took an interest in their personal lives and didn't seem to care about their career plans or development as she was too busy. Penny wasn't shocked to hear this, as she'd received such feedback before and knew she wasn't 'people focused.' What did surprise her was her new manager's attitude. He said that this area of her performance was just as important as the revenue she generated – no one had ever said this to her before.

Evergreen Executive (high energy/ high excellence)

Now that you have a picture of the other three quadrants a leader can work within, you might wonder what makes the Evergreen Executive so different.

The word 'evergreen' is used to symbolise continual, year-round growth. These types of leaders are vibrant, popular and fun to work with – individuals who exude high energy, ensuring that all their interactions are productive and meaningful. They have a genuine interest in others' development and will go out of their way to support the growth of team members and colleagues by making connections or sharing knowledge and expertise freely. This interest in others also extends beyond the workplace, as the Evergreen Executive is authentic and displays consistent behaviour, regardless of whom they're with. They prioritise their well-being and realise the importance of being a good role model when it comes to work-life balance.

Evergreen Executives also deliver exceptional results, and they expect the same from their entire team.

They're clear on what needs to be done. They have a structured approach that involves everyone knowing their roles in accomplishing the desired results. The Evergreen Executive knows the value they bring to anything they're involved in.

As a result of being great with people, processes, customers and strategies, the Evergreen Executive is a leader everyone wants to work with and be led by. People want to be part of their teams. Because a seasoned Evergreen Executive has worked like this for a while, they repeat their methodology in every team they work with, yielding great results. Evergreen Executives get exceptional results, and equally, they care about the people they work with.

Because of their methods, Evergreen Executives have a choice of career options, either within an organisation or in the wider market.

These people can make things look easy. But it's hard work. Effort is required, and this is what the rest of this book is about. To be an Evergreen Executive, you need strong energy and a commitment to professional excellence. Where you place your efforts, where you spend your time, what you need to do differently, what tools you need in your toolkit, and whom you need to spend time with – these are all important considerations moving forward.

As mentioned, Evergreen Executives focus on seven different areas. These seven areas have been split into two groupings, which reflect the vertical and horizontal axes on the matrix above

- Group 1: Personal energy
  - Physical
  - Mental
  - Relationship

- Group 2: Professional excellence
  - Strategy
  - Stakeholders
  - Systems
  - Status

The Evergreen Executive Dashboard, below, is the first tool for your toolkit. It's the ultimate health check. It will tell you where you're starting from and will monitor your progress.

It will be the compass that you can use throughout the rest of your career to ensure you're not neglecting any of these key areas. Over the years, I've observed how inspirational Evergreen Executives are when they keep all these areas in balance. They stay in the green zone as much as possible and take action if they enter the amber or red areas.

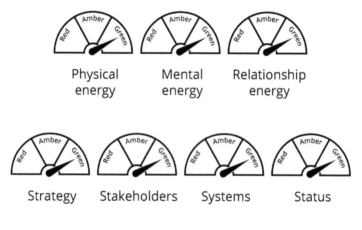

The Evergreen Executive Dashboard

Now we'll look at all seven areas in turn to understand what it takes to perform at this level.

PART ONE
Personal Energy

To operate as a high-performing leader, it's critical to keep your personal energy high. When I think about the leaders I've worked with or worked for, those I remember for the right reasons were enthusiastic, fun to work with, quick thinking, looked the part, and even under high pressure had the energy to help the rest of their team or other parts of the organisation. They had the inner capacity to perform mostly at a high level and were reliable and inspiring. It's impossible to operate in this way unless you feel well and have high energy levels. Indeed, a well-known phrase reminds us that 'we can't give what we haven't got'. As a leader, you're responsible for working with and helping others, and this takes time and energy.

Let's look at how to optimise the energy part of the Evergreen Executive model.

CHAPTER 2

Physical Energy

When we feel physically unwell, we're preoccupied. A serious illness can stop us in our tracks, force us to cancel everything and rest. About six years ago, I kept getting one virus after another but continued working flat out, trying to make myself believe that I was resting when I wasn't. Eventually, blood tests revealed that I had glandular fever. This made complete sense and explained why I'd been feeling so bad for many months. I hadn't listened to my body. It slowed me down so much that I feared something was seriously wrong and asked for more tests. In the end, I had to give up all outside activities, including triathlon racing and training, which I loved, to save the little energy I had left for my work, rest and a healthy recovery.

This was a tough lesson to learn. But now, every time I feel slightly unwell, I no longer push through it. Instead, I rein myself back to ensure a quick recovery and not prolong the energy lapse. My personal tool-kit of resources includes an acupuncturist, massage therapist and trusted doctor who can help me get back on track as soon as possible.

Any client who doesn't take corrective action quickly when the first signs of an illness appear risks making things worse. If they don't take any action at all, they can reach the red zone: complete burnout. This is an unpleasant place to be.

How can you avoid this and keep your physical health as good as possible? Knowing what it feels like to be in a physically good place helps set the standard.

The first step is to develop a clear understanding of what you feel like when you feel well. I can clearly remember waiting for my final diagnostic blood test, after my bout with glandular fever. That same day, I'd met up with a yoga teacher and just finished an intro-ductory one-to-one lesson. As I walked back to my car an hour later, I felt a different sensation physically. And I understood why I felt different: I'd had a glimpse of feeling well again. I'd become so used to feeling unwell that it had become my norm. The feeling I had walking back to my car was the beginning of my journey back to full health. Over the weeks that followed, I experienced more of this sense of well-being and soon that became my new norm. When I realised I'd forgotten what it felt like to feel physically well, I was shocked. I was inspired to keep the practice of yoga in my personal toolkit, and I've been practising daily for seven years now.

Evergreen Executives make it a priority to look after themselves physically. They know that they require consistent levels of energy and a sense of well-being to accomplish their goals inside and outside work while helping others do the same. They inspire others by providing practical support and guidance and modelling good habits and behaviour every day.

Food

You are what you eat (or your energy levels reflect what you eat). For me, this is very true. If I eat poor-quality food, I don't feel well.

Understand what you need to eat to keep your energy levels high.

Leaders who can sustain excellent performance levels over many years eat well most of the time using the 80/20 rule. This means that 80% of the time they eat a nutritious diet and 20% of the time they indulge in treats. Some people I've worked with have always done this, but most have learned the hard way. Because they became ill or felt consistently tired and lacklustre, they turned to nutritional experiments to find out if any food combinations or deficiencies were causing less than optimum energy.

For someone trying to make positive nutritional changes, the office environment can be their worst enemy. Many companies offer treats for birthdays, to get workers through tough deadlines, or as rewards for hard work. Sometimes we think sugar will help us be productive, but it's our worst enemy – it creates a roller coaster of highs and lows.

I didn't realise how much people are affected by sugar until I read *Sweet Poison*, by David Gillespie.[2] The information in this book shocked me, and as a result I've drastically reduced my sugar intake and have seen massive energy benefits. Sugar reliance is

---

2   D Gillespie, *The Sweet Poison Quit Plan: How to kick the sugar habit and lose weight fast* (Penguin, 2013).

one area to investigate if you feel that your energy levels need improving or you're relying on junk food to get through the day.

Similarly, caffeine offers a short-term energy boost but in the long term, it makes you feel worse. I no longer consume any caffeine after midday, so as not to impact my sleep.

Many people turn to alcohol when under pressure professionally and personally or as a reward for hard work, but it also produces peaks and troughs in energy levels.

Zoe and Dan   *Case Study*

One recent client, Zoe, used to drink in the evenings and at weekends. When she reduced her intake to a couple of glasses at the weekend, she noticed a huge, immediate change to her energy levels and now enjoys her stressful job as a leader much more. Another client, Dan, decided to stop drinking entirely. Now he feels a lot better and doesn't miss alcohol at all.

■■■ EXERCISE ■■■

THE EVERGREEN EXECUTIVE DIET

Here are a few questions to consider regarding the nutritional element of your personal energy.

- What food makes you feel energetic?
- What food makes you feel tired?
- What foods do you feel you're eating too much or too little of?
- Are there any eating or drinking habits you'd like to change?

A lot of executives live on a combination of junk food, processed food, sugar, alcohol and caffeine with the excuse that they're too busy to eat properly. The Evergreen Executive isn't among them. They know that they need good energy levels from nutritious food.

Movement

In the modern-day world, many of us move very little. I envy my friends with jobs that demand movement. My running partner is a PE teacher, and whenever we meet, she's already done many more steps than I have simply because she's been walking around all day and teaching classes. I drive to work, walk from the car park to a meeting room, then perhaps to another meeting room, and walk back to the car.

I sit for most of my working day. When I purchased a step counter, I was shocked to learn how little I move. If I don't consciously add more movement into my day, I average only about 4,000 steps. This is well below the somewhat arbitrary recommendation of 10,000 steps a day. There's debate over where this number came from. Some think it was linked to a marketing campaign for a fitness gadget. Regardless, the bottom line is that we could all benefit from being more active.

Our bodies are designed to move around, not sit about all day. Check out the work of Tony Riddle, 'The Natural Life-Stylist', to learn more.[3] Unfortunately

---

3   T Riddle, 'The Natural Life-Stylist', https://tonyriddle.com/, accessed 3 April 2020.

for most employees, their work environments fight against them. Inactivity can eventually impact physical well-being, causing issues such as back aches, joint dysfunction or weight gain. Tony is working to encourage all of us to sit less and move more!

How physically active are you? Being active is another factor in feeling vibrant and having the energy to lead well. Some executives I work with have let their exercise regimes lapse due to work commitments and a lack of time. Long commutes and staying in hotels can impact exercise and movement. But incorporating more movement into your daily routine will make you feel better. Creating new habits, such as parking further away from your destination, or finding specific sports or exercises that you enjoy can increase your physical energy and sense of well-being.

Environment and surroundings

How our surroundings affect our energy levels interests me greatly. Most of us understand how food and physical activity are key to energy and physical well-being. But I hadn't fully considered the impact of our environment and physical surroundings until I learned about minimalism and decluttering. These concepts were made famous recently in Marie Kondo's book *The Life-changing Magic of Tidying*.[4]

Kondo's idea behind minimalism and decluttering is to create a space in which we have only a few things around us that we really need and to organise these things in a systematic way. We then use less energy every day because we have fewer choices to make and can find things more easily.

I've often seen people I've worked with become irritated when they can't find what they're looking for or become stressed out just looking at their desk piled with papers containing things that they need to do. I've seen people arrive at meetings with incorrect or missing information because they couldn't find certain documents. Too much stuff and too many choices can be draining. Perhaps this is another area where you could make some quick improvements to stop your energy from escaping.

Look at your work area. Does it make you feel good and in control? What about when you get home? Does it feel good to sit down in your environment after a hard day,

4   M Kondo, *The Life-changing Magic of Tidying: A simple, effective way to banish clutter forever* (Vermilion, 2014).

or is there something in it that's irritating and preventing that essential recharge? If your space seems untidy, cluttered and stressful, consider these reminders:

- Everything has a place – put everything back where it belongs.
- Throw away anything that's broken, poor quality or no longer of any use or that simply annoys you every time you look at it.
- Only buy things you love.
- Surround yourself at home and work with things that you love and don't irritate you.

When considering your surroundings, don't forget about the outdoors. I run twice a week because it gives me a connection to nature and the seasons, something I don't get from yoga, which I practise indoors. I knew I loved this element of running but didn't realise why until I heard about some research by Professor Richard Taylor on why nature is healing. He says that looking at clouds, trees or raindrops lowers our stress levels because they contain naturally occurring patterns called fractals.[5] Therefore, a simple walk outside at lunchtime or at the weekend could be worth adding to your routine. It's movement that also offers a sense of well-being and reduces stress. Some leaders I know go for a walk after or in between high-intensity meetings to recalibrate, clear their minds and re-energise before going home or returning to the office.

Sleeping patterns

A lot of my clients complain about poor sleep and how a high workload can impact it. Worrying keeps people awake, especially at peak workload times or just after they've returned to work after a holiday. On a recent group holiday, I was shocked to find that one topic of conversation was the apps people were using to get to sleep. The ages of people in the group ranged from twenty-one to sixty-two – and everyone was interested in how to get a good night's sleep.

Matthew Walker, author of *Why We Sleep*, defines inadequate sleep as anything less than a regular seven hours a night.[6] We can all relate to the feeling

---

5   R Taylor, 'Fractal Patterns in Nature and Art Are Aesthetically Pleasing and Stress-reducing', *The Conversation*, 30 March 2017, http://theconversation.com/fractal-patterns-in-nature-and-art-are-aesthetically-pleasing-and-stress-reducing-73255, accessed 3 April 2020.
6   M Walker, *Why We Sleep: The new science of sleep and dreams* (Penguin, 2018).

of not having slept. It isn't a great platform for high-energy performance. If a lack of sleep is an ongoing problem for you, it might be worth trying some sleep-hygiene habits suggested by experts.

The biggest problem I see with leaders is an inability to resist reading emails in the evening. They end up worrying about the contents of these emails and don't sleep well as a result.

MICK   *Case Study*

Mick had a manager who regularly emailed at 11pm or later. The messages were long and often contained demands that needed to be acted on immediately. Eventually, Mick began to dread opening them. He'd lie awake at night worrying about what he was going to do and whether he'd done something wrong. This happened regularly, and because of a lack of sleep, he'd be irritable with his team and colleagues the next day. His wife and young family at home also suffered as a result of his sleepless nights and irritability in the mornings.

It took a long time for Mick to stop reading his emails at night, but eventually he trained himself to not only avoid them after leaving work, but also to not take his work phone on holiday. He left a deputy in charge, asked people to contact this person in regards to anything urgent and set up an out-of-office, re-routing anyone who couldn't wait until his return. It took him a few holidays to get used to this new habit but now, a few years on, Mick wouldn't dream of taking his work phone with him.

Evergreen Executives realise how vital it is to be healthy. They're proactive about their well-being and invest in preventive/alternative treatments. Making time for regular health checks, whether they're free routine ones or privately funded ones, is as important on the to-do list as attending the next management meeting. Leaders who are operating from within another quadrant may not prioritise their physical health enough – action in this area easily falls off the to-do list in times of pressure. But these times are often when such action is needed most.

Over the years, I've added a few things to my well-being kitbag. Today, my health routine includes regular acupuncture and sports massages. If I pick up an injury from running or yoga, I visit a physio sooner rather than later so things don't get worse and result in bigger problems, and I make a deliberate effort to ease back from exercise rather than muscle through, as I've done in the past.

If you're managing a chronic health condition, investing in your well-being is extremely important. I've worked with people with ME, fibromyalgia, autoimmune diseases and chronic fatigue after trauma. Many are inspirational in the way they manage their conditions proactively, and quite often it's impossible to tell that they're juggling an additional health challenge. Finding such role models who proactively manage their conditions could be extremely beneficial if you encounter or already have a similar situation to handle.

Reflection questions

- What is depleting you physically?
- What changes can you make?

- What is replenishing you and making you feel great?

- Are you scheduling enough time for this?

- What else could you do to increase your physical energy?

Where are you starting from?

Using the dial below, rate yourself in this area today.

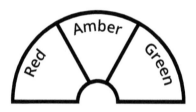

Physical energy

- Green zone – in good shape

- Amber zone – work to be done

- Red zone – immediate action required

CHAPTER 3

Mental Energy

People display high levels of mental energy in various ways. I know when I'm with this type of person. They have a positive outlook on life, they're vibrant and they're mentally engaged in everything that they take on personally and professionally. They have magnetic personalities – they're fun to be around. In my first book, *Own It – Regain Control and Live Life on Your Terms*, they're the Rays of Sunshine characters.

An article written in 2007 by HR Lieberman states that although mental energy is not well defined, it is of substantial public interest. 'Although the physical energy required to complete a task can be objectively specified, the concept of mental energy is relatively new. Mental energy is a mood, but it can also be defined as the ability or willingness to engage in cognitive work.'[7]

---

7   HR Lieberman, 'Cognitive Methods for Assessing Mental Energy', *Nutritional Neuroscience*, Oct–Dec 2007, www.ncbi.nlm.nih.gov/pubmed/18284031, accessed 3 April 2020.

To operate as an Evergreen Executive – to achieve excellent results and inspire others – you must have good mental energy. It's not much fun being part of a team whose leader doesn't have this kind of energy.

We know from the fields of neurolinguistic programming and cognitive behavioural therapy that our thoughts and behaviour are connected. A more recent illustration that links mindset with the growth mindset is presented by Dr Carol S Dweck in her bestseller *Mindset*. A fixed mindset is 'believing that your qualities are carved in stone creating an urgency to prove yourself over and over again'; the 'growth mindset is based on the belief that our basic qualities are things you can cultivate through your efforts, strategies, and help from others'.[8] Operating in the Evergreen Executive way involves having a growth mindset, always aiming to develop new skills and build on your strengths, always learning. As a leader, role-modelling the growth mindset is also important because you lead by example to inspire others. In Chapter 8 of Dr Dweck's book, there is an excellent diagram explaining the differences in behavioural terms for the fixed and growth mindset. This diagram

---

8   Carol S Dweck, *Mindset: Changing the way you think to fulfil your potential* (Random House, 2017).

is a useful tool for the Evergreen Executive leader to use personally and discuss with team members.

This chapter explores ways to maintain high levels of mental energy so that you feel great. Doing so will have a knock-on effect on those you interact with. Optimising your mental energy requires a pick-and-mix approach, just as is the case with your physical energy. You need to find what works for you so that you can embed new habits.

Here are a few that work for me, and for clients and leaders I've worked for.

Purposeful living

Do you feel good about what you do in your job? It's important to be doing something that gives you a feeling of satisfaction, whether it's providing a valuable service, building a product that's of use to someone, improving things, helping people, dedicating yourself to a particular cause or body of research or positively impacting something or someone. As a leader, you must be able to clearly state the value you're adding so that you can inspire others to do the same or to support your activities. Waking up each morning with a clear purpose, knowing you're making a difference in the world, will help you maintain high levels of mental energy.

It's also worth periodically reflecting on how you spent your time over a week or month to ensure that you've been focusing on the right things. It's easy to fall into the trap of being extremely busy but not spending time on things that make you feel good. The Evergreen Executive spends their time wisely, on the right things, and doesn't waste mental energy complaining or getting caught up in things that don't concern them. If you're questioning the value you or your team are adding to an activity or process, evaluate its importance and its impact on others. Sometimes, the corrective action is to stop doing something. There's nothing better than taking an item off your to-do list and feeling relieved that you now have space to work on things that matter to you.

Time for you

On the topic of space, do you take time to do nothing and rest your mind? As a Type-A person, who has a tendency towards being a high-achieving workaholic, I've struggled with this for years. Resting and doing nothing is my biggest challenge. My mind is always overactive, thinking of my to-do list – the number of random thoughts that enter my mind while I'm doing yoga is incredible. And my inability to switch off at night has impacted my sleep over the years.

To address this, I started meditating. I've now been doing it for five years and practising regularly for the last two. I recommend the app Headspace, which contains various meditation programmes. The story of the man behind it, Andy Puddicombe, *Get Some Headspace*, is a good read.[9] I'd always wanted a regular meditation practice, but nothing stuck as a tool in my toolkit until I listened to Bob Roth, a meditation teacher, speaking on a podcast a couple of years ago.[10] As a result, I became intrigued by another form of meditation, Transcendental Meditation, and trained for four days with a local teacher. Over the last eighteen months, I haven't missed a single meditation practice.

In the podcast, Bob Roth used the analogy of plugging a phone into a socket to recharge. That's the

9   A Puddicombe, *Get Some Headspace: 10 minutes can make all the difference* (Hodder Paperbacks, 2011).
10 R Roll, 'Strength in Stillness: Bob Roth on the power of transcendental meditation and bringing calm to the center of life's storm', *The Rich Roll Podcast*, episode 372, 10 June 2018, www.richroll.com/podcast/bob-roth-372, accessed 3 April 2020.

effect meditation has – it reboots and recharges us mentally. My two twenty-minute meditation sessions each day (one on waking and the other at teatime) are now an essential habit that helps me reboot my mental energy and create that mental space I once struggled with. Some organisations are now providing meditation rooms because its proven benefits are being recognised. There are many different types of meditation, so if you're interested in it, it's just a matter of finding one that works for you.

Breadth of interests

Having passions, interests and fun outside work also helps leaders mentally recharge. One leader I worked with was just as passionate about the women's football team she ran as she was about being a senior executive in the top team of a multinational advertising agency. If a leader is operating in the burnout zone, they've let interests outside work go by the wayside. This impacts mental well-being because not only does the person feel guilty for not doing these things, but they also begin to resent their organisation or the pressure from other leaders and peers. This is a downward spiral.

Some of the most interesting Evergreen Executives I've worked with had diverse outside interests, from hot air ballooning and charity work to entertaining and athletics. I'd often hear them have conversations with colleagues or clients that would move on to the subject of the outside interest, and this undoubtedly created a favourable impression with the other party. They'd see the person they were talking to in a more diverse light. Outside passions and interests have two parallel benefits – they offer a mental break and enhance your professional status, showing that you operate on many different levels.

Time to think and plan

Scheduling time to think and plan is another trait of high-performing leaders. This was identified in Stephen R Covey's classic book *The 7 Habits of Highly Effective People*, in the chapter on Habit 3: Put First Things First. He states the importance of making time for activities such as planning, relationship building and recreation.[11] If you want to operate as an Evergreen Executive, it's key to schedule thinking time and to honour it.

---

11 SR Covey, *The 7 Habits of Highly Effective People* (Simon & Schuster, 2004).

One organisation I work with has quiet rooms. If someone is inside the rule is that they can't be interrupted. Some people schedule this time at home. And others find places that make them feel good and go there regularly to recharge and think. Saying that you're too busy for this is unacceptable. Making this time is key to maintaining high mental energy, which leads to optimal performance and personal satisfaction.

Recently I came across a book called *Sabbath*, by Wayne Muller. It made me realise that we've lost a lot of downtime over the past few years since Sunday shopping became the norm and we have technology at our fingertips 24/7. The book reminds us of the benefits of a Sabbath day and suggests ways to create our own Sabbath.[12] Anyone struggling to get mental downtime should add this to their reading list.

To keep your mental energy topped up, you need to recognise when it's beginning to drop and have a habit or tool in your toolkit to use at the earliest opportunity. What are the signs that your mental energy is entering the danger zone? Mine are often physical. I

---

12 W Muller, *Sabbath: Finding rest, renewal, and delight in our busy lives* (Bantam, 2000).

start to feel tired and drained, and the glands in my neck give me a physical reminder that I'm beginning to run on empty.

Another sign is when I have no energy for my daily yoga practice. The old me would have muscled on regardless, but the wiser me cuts practice short and looks at my diary to work out how I can create some alone time and thinking space. This can mean saying no to things or delaying actions or meetings, often without the other person involved noticing or minding. I also know that travelling drains me physically and mentally, so if my work takes me to London or demands a lot of travel, I regularly schedule downtime between appointments. Delivering training workshops, which require 100% focus for many hours, mentally zaps me, so I make time before and after to recharge. My daily meditation practice also helps with this. These are habits I've cultivated over the last five years.

Of course, everyone is different. For example, running an interactive workshop might be mentally energising for more extroverted personalities and have the opposite effect. This type of person might need to schedule time with others to re-energise if they've been locked away working on a report for a week. It's important to design a system where you recognise what's mentally draining for you and come up with tailored solutions to help you recharge.

The word *resilience* is in vogue right now and often stated as a value or core competence. Though the term is overused, it's an important concept to address. I see it as a trait among successful Evergreen Executives. In organisations, as in life, we're constantly challenged by problems, tough situations, difficult people and things we hadn't foreseen. These events drain us mentally and emotionally to the point where staying upbeat can become a challenge. How do you develop the mental resilience to bounce back and not, in coaching terms, get stuck in the pit for too long? The Evergreen Executive needs a few tools in their toolkit to do so. Here are a few techniques:

- Don't respond immediately. Give yourself time to think, especially if you feel attacked and could respond in an emotional, non-professional way. Give it at least twenty-four hours.

- Exercise or do something different away from the situation/person that's draining you mentally. Things are often much clearer when we come back after a break.

- Have a few people in your network whom you can rant to! Talk to someone whose personality is opposite to yours, as they'll see the situation from a completely different perspective.

- Have a few quotes/phrases written down that you can look at to help you put a situation into perspective.

- Listen to a podcast with inspiring hosts and guests. I do this on long journeys or when stuck in traffic to manage mental frustration.

- Have a coffee with a Ray of Sunshine person who will make you laugh and realise that whatever it is will pass.

- Change your environment – go to a place you love and take time out.

- Mix things up by asking yourself if you're feeling mentally stale in regard to some aspect of your role or life and what you could change to add variety and newness. Have you got a scary goal, one that's slightly out of your comfort zone? Focusing on this goal might not be a good strategy if your mental resilience is low, as it could be too much of a challenge, but if boredom is affecting your mental resilience, it might be worth thinking about.

Reflection questions

- Can you clearly state the value your role is adding?

- What are some signs that your mental-energy levels are low?

- How can you reboot your mental energy when you need to?

- Who are your Rays of Sunshine?

Where are you starting from?

Using the dial below, rate yourself in this area today.

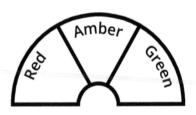

Mental energy

- Green zone – in good shape

- Amber zone – work to be done

- Red zone – immediate action required

CHAPTER 4

Relationship Energy

An inspirational leader must build many effective relationships to deliver exceptional results. This will be explored in the professional excellence part of the book. This chapter focuses on the relationships you need to keep your day-to-day energy levels topped up. Just as they need to make time to look after their physical and mental well-being, the Evergreen Executive also needs to ensure that their relationship and social needs are fulfilled, so that they can inspire others and help them in their development.

The number of personal relationships you need to thrive will vary depending on whether you're more extroverted or introverted. If you're extroverted, you'll need to surround yourself with more people than introverts, who need fewer connections to thrive.

Some connections in our lives are a given, while we have an element of choice in others. For example, you can't choose family members, and you often can't choose a lot of the people you work with, unless you're a hiring manager or self-employed. I ask leaders who are struggling with their energy levels to write down, over the course of a few weeks, whom they spend most of their time with inside and outside of work. We then go through the list and I ask them if each person makes them feel energised or drained after an interaction.

One manager I worked with recently was shocked to realise how few people energised him – no wonder he was struggling to inspire others at work. We immediately began addressing this. I asked him to think hard and remember the people he'd encountered in the past or still spent time with occasionally who were good to be around. The plan was for him to reconnect with some of those people he'd lost contact with and increase the amount of time with newer connections who had similar traits.

People migrate to people who are similar to them. High-energy people like being around other high-energy people. Normally, if you tap into one person, by default you also tap into their connections. High-energy people also keep in touch with other high-energy people, as the effect is mutually beneficial.

The Generation Sandwich

One challenge facing a lot of senior leaders is the Generation Sandwich, which can be an energy drain and a massive time commitment requiring heavy diary management.

The Generation Sandwich

This is when you find yourself responsible for older family members with failing health or emotional needs, your own immediate family and sometimes grandchildren. All these parties have different needs that require you to play different roles in addition to your role as a leader. It's not unusual in one day to accompany a parent to a hospital appointment, present a key pitch to a senior management team and attend a son or daughter's graduation ceremony. But perhaps a stepchild also wants you to attend a parents' afternoon. If you're unable to attend because of your other commitments, you may feel a cocktail of guilt. You might worry about whether you're letting people down, about how you'll be perceived and about favouritism accusations. This can lead to mental exhaustion.

But the positive side of this challenge is that when peers and subordinates face similar situations, you'll have immediate empathy.

Another pull on your relationship-energy levels may be activities inside or outside work that demand your time alongside your formal role as a leader. Certain requests can accompany the Generation Sandwich as you become more visible in your role. You could be asked to become a member of a parent–teacher association or a fundraising committee, a coach of a child's sports team, or a member of the social committee at work. You might be asked to be a link to the external community, to bridge the gap between business and customers. You might become involved in your professional body and perhaps mentor more junior members of staff. You might have village commitments. The list is endless.

The key thing to be aware of is when these activities and commitments stop being fun, energising additions to your life and start feeling like draining obligations that you resent. Some are short-term commitments, but many are huge time-stealers that become difficult to detach from.

If you're spread too thin and your personal energy levels are running on empty, you might need to make tough choices to avoid entering physical and/or mental danger zones. A relationship can bring our energy levels down, it can have a neutral effect or it can increase our energy, so it's important to manage this aspect of the personal energy cocktail as best as you can.

■■■ EXERCISE ■■■

WHO ENERGISES YOU?

Generate a list of people whom you've spent time with over the last month. Divide the list into two groups – those who gave you energy and those who took it away.

Energy takers

Energy takers can have many names, including saboteurs, life victims and negative colleagues. I call them Dark Storms. Other names I've heard are drains or mood hoovers, but you get the idea. If you want to operate in the Evergreen Executive quadrant, you need to limit your time with these people. If any show up on your social media feeds, I suggest muting them, as every post of theirs you read will zap your personal energy. It's normally impossible to completely avoid these people, especially if they're in a work team or in your family. This is where managing boundaries and limiting the time you spend with them becomes important in terms of optimising your personal energy.

Energy givers

Energy givers are important to us, and we must strive to be like them. An Evergreen Executive is certainly an energy giver. Let's look at two important energy-giving characters.

Supporters: How many people genuinely believe in you and want you to succeed professionally and personally? That's the good thing about the work I do – I get paid to support people when I am hired as their coach. Do you have a mentor or a go-to person who can fulfil this role? If not, make it a priority to find someone. This person needs to give you energy and inspire you. Have a think about people who impress you, either in your current workplace or in places you've worked before. You may have met someone socially and felt there was a professional compatibility. If it's someone you worked with a long time ago, this doesn't matter – if the relationship was once strong, it will be easy to reconnect and rebuild.

Time spent with people like this is time well spent, and the time you spend with them doesn't have to be long. Touching base with them occasionally can massively increase your energy levels. My personal coach plays this role for me, and it doesn't even take an hour. It can be a fifteen-minute call or a simple WhatsApp voice note – his preferred method of communication because it's quicker than typing!

Role models: These are people who live and breathe the qualities and behaviour you want to exhibit, and they also keep your personal energy levels high. They're real-life examples of why you're doing what you're doing. Being an Evergreen Executive is hard work, but the rewards are massive, and these people demonstrate this when you interact. How many do you know and how often do you interact with them? Are they on that list of people that you put together earlier? Role models are normally busy because they're successful and people want to spend time with them, but they also have a lot of energy and a huge capacity for work due to exceptional time-management and organisational skills. As these role models also like to interact with high-energy people, they won't mind spending time with you. They love seeing others develop.

Supporters and role models can be any age, come from any background and work in any industry. What they have in common is a state of mind and an attitude that means they take a natural, genuine interest in other people's well-being, work and family life, while also remaining committed to excellence in everything they do. Several of the energy givers in my support network are many years younger than I am, and I find them inspiring to spend time with. The Evergreen Executive continues to grow and learn, always looking for opportunities to evolve, and this takes a high-energy mindset. Remember the Danger Zone and At Risk quadrants. If you surround yourself with people who operate in these quadrants, you could end up in them yourself, thinking you can continue doing the same thing even as the world evolves.

Behaviour breeds behaviour, and a senior leader I was coaching recently had to work hard in this area. They found themselves among a senior management team where over 50% of the people operated in these quadrants. They began to dread each interaction and the monthly leadership meeting. Realising that they were becoming drawn into this way of thinking, they called me and asked for my help managing their professional boundaries with these peers so they could maintain their own high standards of performance regardless of their surrounding environment. We put together an action plan that involved seeking out and spending time with supporters and role models.

Finally, one important relationship that we might neglect is our relationship with ourselves. In his book *Digital Minimalism*, Cal Newport reminds us that we all need solitude to function correctly and that in this era of constant technology, it can be difficult to carve out. He suggests ways to reconnect with the act of solitude.[13] In my own life, I'm trying to be more disciplined with technology so that I get the downtime I need to maintain my personal energy levels. When we're plugged in all the time, we don't allow ourselves to spend time being comfortable with just ourselves.

Reflection questions

- With whom are you spending most of your time? Consider the list you made earlier.

- What is the balance of energy givers and energy takers in your life?

- How are you managing boundaries, especially in relationships where you have little choice, for example, with family members or people you have to work with?

---

13 C Newport, *Digital Minimalism: Choosing a focused life in a noisy world* (Penguin, 2019).

Where are you starting from?

Using the dial below, rate yourself in this area today.

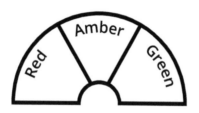

Relationship energy

- Green zone – in good shape
- Amber zone – work to be done
- Red zone – immediate action required

Personal Energy Wrap-up

We've looked at the components of personal energy and how it's important to look after all three: physical energy, mental energy and relationship energy. How are the dials looking? You don't have to wait until you've finished the book to act.

Leaders in the At Risk quadrant make the mistake of seeing personal energy as a poor second in terms of importance compared to their massive professional to-do lists. Personal energy is just as important (if not more so) as professional excellence because if you don't look after your personal well-being, you won't be able to demonstrate professional excellence, or if you do, it won't be sustainable.

What quick wins can you achieve now? What new habits can you integrate into your life to get those dials to green? If they're already green, keep doing what you're doing and read on!

If you need to do a lot of work, identify one small change in each of the following categories:

- To increase your physical energy
- To increase your mental energy
- To increase your relationship energy

PART TWO

Professional Excellence

Now we move on to the business side of being at the top of your game as a leader.

This part of the book will enable you to build a toolkit of processes that you can continually refine and repeat in any role, industry or organisation, regardless of size.

It will enable you to deliver the right results individually and also harness the resources of your people to collectively create a high-performing team.

CHAPTER 5

Strategy

A strategy is a plan of action designed to achieve a long-term aim.

A well-thought-out strategy, which can be communicated simply to all stakeholders, is fundamental to professional excellence. It allows a leader to align time and resources with top-level organisational direction. It ensures that everybody knows where they fit in. It can be motivational for all players to see how their day-to-day activities contribute to the bigger picture. In large organisations, there's often a feeling of disconnection within certain departments and roles when individuals can't see the point of the day-to-day work they're doing.

Some large organisations have sophisticated processes for setting top-level strategies and cascading these down throughout. Over the past thirty-five years, I've seen extremely complex strategic-planning documents and very simple ones. The worst situation is when there's no plan at all. An Evergreen Executive puts together one of their own.

When I worked at Hewlett Packard in the 1980s and 1990s, every manager used a ten-step business-planning process. In the annual business plan, the next financial year was described in great detail, the following three years were outlined and the fifth year was addressed in a general capacity. The detailed one-year plan was then used as a management tool to identify any areas that were behind schedule/off plan, so that we could take the appropriate corrective action. Each manager had to set up charts that measured key processes and key performance indicators (KPIs) monthly using a traffic-light system: green (okay, in control), amber (beware, heading out of control), red (out of control, urgent action needed). Everyone was trained in the process and it was required of every leader.

If you work for an organisation with a clear, cascaded plan like this, you'll need to familiarise yourself with the process and create your own team plan in the required format. You'll then need to communicate your plan to all team members, senior leaders and stakeholders that you work alongside. It will be critical to your success to run this process like clockwork and motivate your team to own their individual elements, as well as to develop corrective-action plans for any areas that aren't running smoothly. These plans will be your master-control documents and act as a compass. They'll show you how your team is performing and contributing to the company's overall goal. If this sounds familiar to you, I'm guessing that you have this part of the professional toolkit under control.

That being said, some leaders forget its importance when they move to a new organisation that doesn't have such a defined process. They quickly find themselves in the firefighting mode that becomes very stressful over time. If this rings a few bells, it might be good to dig out any documents you have on how you built your own strategic plan in previous roles.

The worst situation that leaders find themselves in is when the company they work for doesn't have a clearly defined, cascaded annual-planning process and they've never worked with anyone who uses this approach. If this is you, you're probably lost by now.

Don't worry, it's simple to create your own plan – and it's worth investing the time to create one. We're going to tackle this now.

I do know some entrepreneurs who've never had a plan and have seen their businesses grow organically, but this option is a risky one.

A plan on a page

I challenge you to start thinking about building a strategic twelve-month plan for your area of responsibility that, ideally, you can fit on one side of A4 paper. You can create your 'strategic plan on a page' using templates you build yourself or that your organisation has provided. See Appendix 1 at the back of this book or visit www.sandrawebbercoaching.com/books to download a strategic plan on a page template to get you started, but please do adapt it to work for you – this is just an example.

Your plan on a page might include:

- Your team's overall purpose
- How your team links into the overall business
- Your personal vision for the team (think step changes/breakthroughs)

- Short-, medium- and long-term goals
- Projects you're involved in
- Key processes you're responsible for
- Areas where processes need to be established or improved
- All areas of internal and external accountability
- People-development planning
- Company-wide values or core competencies
- KPIs (if not given to you, consider creating your own and flagging them green/amber/red) and their defining criteria
- A way of depicting your plan so that you can communicate it with power – graphical, cartoon, tabular, mind map
- How your plan can evolve if things change
- How you can measure whether you're on track
- How you can assign ownership to others

Start by writing down the components of your plan. Then establish whether there are any natural groupings that will lead to a structure for your plan that makes sense to you (assuming you aren't using an organisational template).

Then, think about the outputs you need to achieve personally and your entire team's responsibility. If there are any critical, fixed deadlines that have been dictated externally, place these in your twelve-month plan. For any other projects, estimate timescales and completion deadlines. When your plan starts to make sense and take shape, think about who the sub-owners of each activity are and who in your team could manage project and process ownership other than you.

Before you go any further, check in with your senior manager to make sure that you're clear about the higher-level strategic direction and what's required of you and your team, be that a team reporting directly to you or virtual teams that you lead. It's becoming increasingly common for virtual teams to be created for specific purposes. A high-performing leader must be able to operate with these teams. The good thing is that all the elements of the toolkit in this section, including this strategic planning, apply equally to traditional teams and temporary virtual-based ones.

After writing the initial draft, it might be worth testing the layout with someone in your team or a mentor who can provide critical input regarding what makes sense and what needs more work. At this stage, the person reviewing it will likely come up with things you've missed – we're often too close to our subject matter and can benefit from an independent eye. It's crucial that your plan on a page captures everything you're accountable for in your organisation.

Once you've reviewed the plan with a trusted person, it's time to share your thinking with the wider team. If there are other managers or team leaders in your department, get their input up front to ensure that you've captured everything they're responsible for. The acid test will be whether they're happy to step up and repeat the process with their teams. Have you created a template that everyone can use and understand? These cascaded plans on a page will be key communication tools for line management and stakeholder management.

The ongoing process you create should consist of:

- Devising your plan on a page every year and reviewing it on a quarterly basis to ensure completeness
- Updating it monthly with progress against the plan (some items might need only quarterly updates) using the monthly dashboard process outlined in Chapter 7.

New to your role

If you're changing roles, it might be useful to read *The First 90 Days*, by Michael D Watkins. Chapter Six has some great tips on gaining alignment, which will help you formulate your plan on a page.[14] If you're completely new to a role, an organisation or both, it makes sense to use the initial three months (hence the common term 'ninety-day planning') to collect information and build an understanding of the role you now have, your organisation's culture, your managers' key priorities and your team's health. You may also want to get input from stakeholders. Be curious during these initial few months. Find out what's working well and identify short- and long-term issues that need fixing. Gather data systematically. You'll use your findings and information from other parties when formulating your plan on a page. Even if you just record your findings in a notebook, this will ensure that you can build a 360-degree picture of what you need to focus on as a leader.

When you've got used to building these plans on a page to suit your individual leadership style, this

---

14 MD Watkins, *The First 90 Days: Proven strategies for getting up to speed faster and smarter* (Harvard Business Review, 2013).

initial data-gathering phase will also become systematic. You may generate a list of considerations that you address every time you build a new plan on a page, such as:

- Senior management team requirements
- Team requirements
- Your personal vision
- Stakeholder requirements
- Current strengths, weaknesses, opportunities and threats (SWOT) analysis of your team

After the initial three months, start downloading the key themes and identifying people to whom you can eventually delegate ownership.

Keeping your plan alive

We've all fallen into the trap of building a plan, whether it be inside or outside of work, being enthusiastic about it and then eventually forgetting about it. Some people are naturally good at generating ideas, while others devise great plans or ensure that things are implemented to completion.

As a leader in charge of this strategic plan on a page, you're responsible for making sure that everything gets done in line with the agreed plan. Of course, you can delegate a lot of specific activities and, indeed, large subsections of the plan to those you report directly to. They, in turn, can cascade it down to their teams. But it's your responsibility to ensure that your master plan, once finalised, becomes a useful business tool both for yourself and all your stakeholders, including your team. This plan should make everyone's life easier and allow you all to focus on the right things without getting side-tracked.

Many leaders I've worked with get easily bogged down in the day-to-day running of their teams and can't find the time to get out of firefighting mode, a reactive way of working that leads to low team morale, stress and deteriorating performance levels. They feel as if they're on a hamster wheel every day of every week with no way out.

MELANIE

Melanie was in this exact situation when I started working with her. She'd been heading up a customer-service team for a few years, having worked her way up from customer-service assistant to team leader and eventually head of department. She came to our first session frustrated because she felt out of control. During a recent performance review, she'd been rated 'just below acceptable' for the first time in her career. She loved her job and couldn't understand why her personal performance rating had deteriorated when she was working so hard and also pushing her team to its limits just to keep up with the work coming into her department.

We spent the first couple of sessions getting clarity on her team's roles and responsibilities, her company's organisational structure, the processes she owned completely and the ones that her team were involved in but didn't own in their entirety. We also determined that she needed to have a frank discussion with her manager about the KPIs that he held her responsible for and the performance levels he expected for each.

As Melanie pieced together this information, she constantly felt guilty about not helping her team enough with the day-to-day firefighting in the department. As her coach, my job was to reassure her that taking time out to build a solid plan regarding what needed to be done to get out of firefighting mode would help her and her team in the long run. I also had to hold her accountable for scheduling time to gather data, think about and document a plan of action, and talk to her team members about this new approach.

When her plan was complete, Melanie assigned operational tasks and longer-term breakthrough projects to her four team leaders, who, in turn, used the same approach with their direct reports. Melanie started to review her master plan on a page with her line manager once a month and built it into her one-to-one discussions with her team leaders each month. It took six months for this process to become normal, but the team leaders and Melanie started to see the benefits of getting operational, day-to-day tasks under control and working on large-scale improvement projects in parallel. The projects were no longer seen as unachievable as they were more integrated into the working week rather than viewed as add-ons.

Integrating your plan into other processes

Firstly, as the plan's owner (and as a leader), you must walk the talk. Everyone needs to see that you're using the plan yourself and that everything you do relates back to this master document. This means that you must always have it to hand. But practically, how can you do this? What do you carry with you when you're in meetings, having discussions with your direct reports, sitting down with your manager or visiting external customers or suppliers? What do you take with you when you're travelling on business or when you're at conferences? Do you have a daybook? Do you work electronically and keep everything on a laptop? Your plan needs to be associated with you as a high-performing executive. People need to see that this is the way you ensure that you're delivering on all things. It needs to be in a practical, mobile format, not something hidden within a PowerPoint slide or on a chart fixed to the wall of the office and nowhere else.

What works for me is a master electronic copy in Excel or Word that can be easily exported into presentation format or printed out to carry around. One manager I worked with had his plan on a page mapped out on a huge laminated sheet of paper. He was known for walking around the office complex with this paper under his arm! Think about how you work naturally and how you can create a version of your plan that fits into your way of working. Decide on how to periodically review and update the master version. This could happen monthly or quarterly, depending on how much change occurs within your area of responsibility. Consider the plan's physical format first.

Next, refer to your plan regularly, talking to your manager and direct reports. They need to be familiar with the format so they can see how it fits in with their roles. If there's a standard company format available, this will make things easier because the concept will be familiar to all. If there isn't, you need to create one. Every time people meet with you, they should see you refer to your plan.

Reflection questions

- Do you already have a plan that you need to start using?

- If you need to build a plan from scratch or update an older one, have you got all the inputs you need?

- Is the format right?

- Have you got a list of people in your own team or integrated stakeholders that you work closely with to whom you can assign ownership?

Suggested next steps

Set aside some time to build your plan.

Where are you starting from?

Using the dial below, rate yourself in this area today.

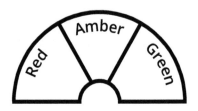

Strategy

- Green zone – in good shape

- Amber zone – work to be done

- Red zone – immediate action required

CHAPTER 6

Stakeholders

The second element in the professional excellence toolkit is learning how to effectively manage the various stakeholders who are relevant to your current role. A stakeholder is anyone with an interest or concern in the activities you're ultimately held responsible for. They're key to helping you achieve the plan you set out in the previous chapter. To identify your relevant stakeholders, you'll first need complete clarity on your own role and what's expected of you over the short, medium and long term. This role clarification is also a prerequisite for completing your strategic plan on a page, which we looked at in the previous chapter.

There are two different methods you can use to build a picture of your stakeholders, assess the relative importance and current health of each relationship, and then note any necessary actions:

1. Draw a diagram so that you have a pictorial representation, which I refer to as a stakeholder map (see Appendix 2 for an example)

2. Create an Excel or Word table that gives an overview of this information and can act as a tool for communicating with others

How to identify your stakeholders

The easiest way to identify your personal stakeholders is to consider your role and then list (or draw a diagram of) anyone inside or outside your organisation who will be impacted by what you do and anyone you need to work with to carry out your role. Here are some people who might be on your list:

- Direct reports and other team members
- Your line manager
- Other senior managers whose team is either an internal customer or a supplier of your key processes and deliverables

- Anyone who pulls together data that your team provides
- Customers who are impacted by you and your team
- Internal staff who need information from you or provide you with information
- Outside legal entities you interface with
- Professional bodies or organisations to which you belong
- Auditors
- Members of project teams you belong to
- Third parties who are critical to your success

Each individual role will have a different set of stakeholders. Every time you move into a new role, you'll need to work through this exercise and prepare a new list. If you're lucky enough to receive a handover from the person previously in your role, ask them for the names of key people they interfaced with before building your own list.

Assessing the importance and health of your stakeholder relationships

Once you have your list, you'll need to develop a process to actively manage the stakeholders, to ensure that you develop effective two-way relationships whereby both parties' needs are met and the work is simultaneously productive, efficient and fun!

First, analyse where you're starting from. Rank each stakeholder on your list from 1 to 10 in terms of how important your relationship with them is to your success in your role. For example:

- The relationship between you and your line manager would be a 10 (of critical importance).

- The relationship between you and your direct reports would be a 10.

- The relationship between you and your peers on the senior management team could be an 8 (important), but you might feel that some relationships within the team are more important than others – use the rating scale of 1–10 to illustrate the relative importance.

- Some customer relationships might be a 9 (very important) while others may be less so and have scores of 3–5.

The ratings will be entirely subjective, based on your experience within your role or input from others if you're new to your role. When rating each of your stakeholder's importance, try to be pragmatic – don't give each of them a 10. A scattering of importance levels will help if you have to prioritise work in the future because you and your team are overloaded.

At this stage, it might be useful to ask someone you work with, who has a good appreciation of your role, to look at your list. A few years ago, I was facilitating a senior-executive team meeting. After everyone had built their stakeholder lists, they asked other team members to offer feedback. One team member took great pleasure in pointing out that a peer had missed a critical stakeholder in his diagram – the department that was managed directly by the team member giving the feedback!

As mentioned earlier, getting an external perspective on our work is extremely valuable because we're often too close to it and can't see the obvious. Ask a few people to look over your list to make sure it represents every facet of your role.

The next step in building your stakeholder list or map (see Appendix 2 or visit www.sandrawebbercoaching. com/books to download an example), is to assess the health of the relationships between you and your stakeholders. Use the same scoring system as you did when analysing the importance of each stakeholder. And be honest, even if the numbers aren't what you want to see.

The final stage is then to take a look at your stakeholder overview and review what action needs to be taken to improve any relationships. Your focus should be on those stakeholders that are of high importance and currently have a low relationship health score. For these relationships, an owner (either yourself or a team member) needs to be assigned the action of improving the health of the relationship moving forwards.

To summarise, here are the four steps:

1. List all stakeholders
2. Rate each stakeholder (between 1 and 10) in terms of their importance to your role

3. Rate each stakeholder (between 1 and 10) in terms of the current health of your relationship with them

4. Identify where your actions should be focused and who should take ownership of these actions within your team

What typically happens at this stage is that a few stakeholders will jump off the page, especially if they received a high score in terms of importance but a low score in terms of relationship health.

You need to prioritise improving these relationships.

DANIEL   *Case Study*

Daniel had been in his finance leadership role for about six months when he learned about stakeholder mapping. He was pleased that he could build a comprehensive list and easily rate the importance of his stakeholders. The difficulties started when he rated the health of his relationships with his stakeholders with honesty – he gave some of his team members and peers low scores. Some of these people he hadn't spent a lot of time with and didn't really know, while others were people whom he didn't naturally connect with (based on first impressions or because they had different ways of working). For Daniel, this exercise was a mirror that showed him he needed to put in time and effort to get to know these people better and maybe adapt some of his ways of working to build better, more effective working relationships.

How to start making improvements

Here are some ways you can start improving the health of your relationships with stakeholders.

- Be curious – adopt an attitude of curiosity and ask questions to understand the other party.

- Strive for win-win – aim to make sure you're both benefiting from the relationship by finding out what each party needs for success.

- Get clarity – understand exactly what deliverables are needed, and in what format and by when.

- Understand personalities – find the similarities and respect the differences so that you can tailor communications.

- Understand motivations – try to assess what motivates the person so you can tap into this (especially important for direct reports in your team).

- Be assertive – don't be afraid to challenge others' thinking and ideas and to have others challenge you.

- Negotiate – make concessions where necessary to move forward.

Now let's look at how you can use these suggestions to build highly effective relationships with specific types of stakeholders who are likely to be on the list you've just created.

Managing upwards

This is often referred to as 'managing your manager' and is a useful skill to learn. Do you feel curious about how each manager operates and their style of leadership? How do they react under pressure? Are they consistent or random? Do they have any hot buttons – behaviours or subjects that get an emotional reaction?

Some managers might be passionate or sensitive. Others might have fixed views and be difficult to influence. Become a data-gathering detective. Learn about each of your key senior manager stakeholders. Work out which part of your natural communication style works well with theirs and where you might need to adapt to improve your working relationship. Tweaking your approach to optimise every working relationship you have without compromising the quality of what you do is a real skill. If you're struggling with a leader, observe whom they seem to work well with and see if there's anything you can learn from their behaviour.

As an executive coach and also as a career coach, one sentence I hear often is 'I don't get on with my manager and I'm thinking of leaving.' In this situation, the first thing that needs to be done is to consider some of the suggestions above to identify the points of difference. Sometimes, a few tweaks in terms of communication can make all the difference and prevent a knee-jerk career decision that might not be in your best interests. Sometimes the differences are too big to work around, but you won't know this until you get out of a victim-and-blame mentality, which is easy to fall into if you've been frustrated for months or years by the situation.

Adopting a win-win mindset can also help in this situation. How can you give the senior-leadership stakeholders you work with a win? By helping them achieve their professional results and getting completely clear on the information or deliverables they need from you and your team in order to succeed. Aligning yourself and your team around these key issues will enhance your reputation for working on the right things and delivering results.

This leads into the next point – getting clarity. This is extremely important in all your work as a high-performing leader. If you don't know what's required, be brave and ask for more information assertively. Know what needs to be achieved.

TED   *Case Study*

One of my clients, Ted, was struggling with his manager. After every one-to-one discussion, he tried to work out whether he'd understood things correctly. Weeks later, he'd find out that he'd been working on the wrong things, and his manager began to wonder whether he could do the job he'd been hired to do. Ted had been successful in all his previous roles and had managed large numbers of people in customer-care teams, so he was confident in his abilities and couldn't work out why he was in this situation. He was beginning to doubt his capabilities.

I asked Ted what happened in the one-to-one discussions, and it became apparent that his manager was vague about what he wanted Ted to focus on and kept changing the priorities at every meeting. The discussions weren't being documented, so Ted often wondered whether he'd misheard something, despite knowing he had a good memory.

We started to explore what Ted could do differently to 'manage his manager'.

He began taking notes at each meeting so that he could clarify the agreed areas of focus in an email afterwards. His manager could then let him know if there was any misunderstanding. Ted also started taking the email summary of the previous meeting into his next one-to-one and updated it if anything changed or wasn't mentioned. He had to build up the confidence to have challenging conversations with his manager, to get clarity, but a trail of key projects developed. After six months, Ted developed his own plan on a page for his team. This doubled as a working document that he used to ensure he was working on the right things in the eyes of his manager.

He worked like this for a year, and during his next appraisal, his performance was rated as good and was no longer in question. In fact, he mentored other individuals working for the same manager, and they adopted a similar approach – they had a working document to use as a tool to ensure that they were focusing on the right things.

This scenario illustrates what can happen when there's a big difference in personality type between you and your senior stakeholders and what you need to do to adapt your approach. In Ted's case, his manager would talk at length in a scattergun way about what he wanted Ted to do, but Ted needed short, sharp, specific actions that could go on a to-do list or that he could use to build a project plan. His manager was never going to work in this way, as it wasn't his natural style, so Ted had to take his manager's ideas and creativity and formulate them into something he could work with while also checking that he hadn't missed anything critical or new at various key points.

Leaders who are natural creative types often change their minds if they think of something better but fail to communicate this to people working on the subject matter. Often, this oversight isn't intentional

– they just have a spontaneous way of working. If it isn't your way, it can be frustrating unless you adopt techniques similar to Ted's.

Your team

The Evergreen Executive must also be able to quickly create a high-performing team. The more times you have to do this, the more it will become a step-and-repeat process. It will become second nature.

This subset in a leader's stakeholder list is of vital importance. If you've rated it less than 10 in terms of relationship health, it might be worth reassessing. In one of my recent coaching sessions, the practical impact of not investing in this group of people was evident.

PETE   *Case Study*

Pete was a senior member of a technical-quality team to which a new leader had been appointed six months ago. The team, including Pete, had been excited about their new leader, who had great credentials and a good reputation in the industry. The first few weeks went well. The new leader was people focused and made a good first impression. But six months later, the situation was very different. The new leader was rarely available and always in meetings. The one-to-ones hadn't continued. (In Chapter 7, we'll look at this issue closely.)

When Pete and his peers did get time with their leader, the meetings started late and were unstructured. Each person felt that they didn't get any time to talk about important issues. The team also felt that there was unclear communication as to who was responsible for what. This was leading to a duplication of efforts and to errors that impacted other important stakeholders in the team. The new leader had quickly become caught up in the company culture of organisational chaos and had already lost his team's respect.

The leader fell into the trap of neglecting this group of stakeholders because they were close to home. It's a mistake to assume that your team is fine simply because people have been in their roles for a long time and know what they're doing. You need to check in with all your stakeholders regularly and dedicate focused time to meaningful one-to-one conversations with them. Your direct reports should be top priority. From my perspective as a high-performance coach, I think everyone should have a meaningful one-to-one conversation with their manager at least once a month about subjects other than their to-do list items.

If an individual working in a routine role is performing well and highly motivated, you might be able to hold the one-to-one meetings once every quarter, but that's the maximum amount of time a leader should leave between these meetings. Sit down with each direct report and check that they're on the right track, working on the right things and getting the feedback and support they need. You should also find out if there's anything else they need from you as their leader.

In the chapter on systems, I'll share an idea for a standard structure that you can use for this type of conversation. You can use it as it is or adapt it to suit your style and role. It's key to invest time in getting to know your team members' personalities and motivations, and to be clear on what you hold team members accountable for. The worst consequence of neglecting this critical group of stakeholders is coming in one day to find that a valuable team member has unexpectedly handed in their resignation – especially if you know that with more attention, this might have been prevented.

Peers and developing the internal-customer mindset

If you take a helicopter view of your stakeholder list, you'll see many names in this category. Key processes or deliverables will require you to work with peers. When one party supplies information to or relies on input from another, it's important that both parties have complete clarity on what's required, when and in what format.

When I worked for Hewlett Packard, we were all trained in process management and continuous improvement. In those days, we called it total quality control. All leaders were sent on in-depth training and were expected to adopt a mindset of continual improvement within their respective teams. As a result, many of our individual performance-related goals centred around improving existing key processes, which had defined process owners, or setting up new processes to improve the overall external customer experience.

We were trained to spend time mapping out the current process. In most of the process mapping, the information/data passed between individuals, teams or departments. The whole process could work effectively only if each part of the chain delivered what the other parts needed to do their bit of work. Each deliverable had to be of a certain quality and delivered in the right timeframe (ie right the first time)! If this wasn't achieved, there would be a rework, which would add extra costs, or a substandard deliverable. We were encouraged to think of these internal partners as internal customers and approach other departments with the same high standards as we would approach an external one.

Ask yourself these questions: Do I have this internal-customer mindset? Do all my team members understand it?

KNOW YOUR AUDIENCE

Case Study

This approach recently came up in a discussion I had with the managing director of a small company. He suddenly realised that his entire workforce had no idea what he'd been talking about when he'd reminded them at a recent company meeting to focus on internal-customer relationships. He'd worked for a large corporation and had had similar training to mine but none of his workforce had, so it was impossible for them to understand the concept. We're now embarking on some basic process-management and continuous-improvement training to help make sure all leaders understand the power of having clearly defined processes, with identified process owners, and ensure everyone is encouraged to continually look for ways of optimising these processes to improve efficiency and effectiveness.

Sometimes it's worth asking whether the other party knows what 'good' looks like. If they don't, training or mentoring is required so that the standard can be set and everyone knows what the end goal is.

External partners and customers

When building effective relationships with external parties, be they private clients, businesses, auditors, suppliers or professional bodies, you need to take a genuine interest in identifying what they require from you, so their needs are met. You also need to be clear on what you need from them in order to meet their expectations. The aim is to exceed these expectations. We've all visited a hotel or a restaurant where we had a faultless experience. We probably tell a lot of our friends and family about it. Such experiences should be treasured, and the Evergreen Executive should use them as fuel to strive for something similar. They should ask themselves and the teams they lead how they can exceed their customers' expectations. This is the mindset we need to adopt.

When I was a finance manager, auditors visited the company regularly. My aim was always to build a good relationship with the auditor by getting to know their personality type and by taking an interest in them, their organisation and the process we were both involved in.

Once you've established a solid relationship with your stakeholders, whether internal or external, you can work with them to resolve any problem that might arise. The projects I worked on with colleagues from different areas of the business, or other external parties, were some of the most rewarding. When you achieve outstanding results together, you see a perfect illustration of a high-performing team in action, with all individuals knowing they contributed towards a great result.

Reflection questions

- Can you list all your internal and external stakeholders?

- Have you had this list reviewed to make sure it's complete?

- Have you created a simple summary in diagram or table form that you can use to assess the relative importance and current health of your relationships with these stakeholders?

- Do you know the key stakeholders with whom you want to improve your relationship? And do you have a plan of action to achieve this? Have you transferred some of the items in this plan to your current to-do list? (If you don't know the quality of your relationship with a particular stakeholder, ask them for feedback).

Suggested next steps

- Draft your stakeholder map (see Appendix 2 or visit www.sandrawebbercoaching.com/books for an example – but choose a format that suits you).
- Review this map with another person.

Where are you starting from?

Using the dial below, rate yourself in this area today.

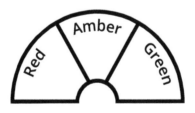

Stakeholders

- Green zone – in good shape
- Amber zone – work to be done
- Red zone – immediate action required

CHAPTER 7

Systems

This chapter outlines a methodology to simplify your responsibilities as a leader. I want you to create a set of management processes that you can take with you into any role and that become second nature. I work with a lot of leaders who are struggling because they haven't developed this important piece of their toolkit. Leading people and creating high-performing teams who consistently generate above-average results should be systematic, to make your life easy, and it should involve taking people with you on a fun journey in which you all enjoy working together. Some of the best leaders I've worked for and coached make this look easy.

In this chapter, I'll outline seven management processes to execute daily. Combined, these components will give you a leadership system.

- Process 1: Set clear direction via a plan on a page
- Process 2: Manage stakeholders effectively
- Process 3: Create a monthly dashboard
- Process 4: Define roles and responsibilities
- Process 5: Maximise people's potential
- Process 6: Optimise your time
- Process 7: Stay current

The aim is that once you've created these processes and used them for a while, they'll become so embedded in your daily life that even when you're going through professional or personal challenges, you'll keep them going.

Let's look at each one in turn, starting with the two that we've already covered in some detail.

Management process 1: Set clear direction via a plan on a page

You should always be able to communicate your personal vision for your team, and this vision should be supported by long-, medium- and short-term goals. Ideally, this vision should be presented on one page and in a portable, professional format so that it can be shown to any of your stakeholders at any time. It should include three things:

1. Your team's purpose (ie what it's responsible for)
2. Where you want to take your team (ie a clear picture of the future)
3. The actions required by you and your team members to ensure excellence in day-to-day operations and achieve a future vision

After developing this plan, you need to keep it alive via communication and updates to ensure that it reflects any changes in the business. Plans quickly lose their credibility if they aren't used or communicated, or if they're irrelevant. Your job as an Evergreen Executive is to make sure that your plan is impactful, exciting, achievable and understood. If you aren't working for an organisation with a system in place that you simply bolt into, you can capitalise on your individuality – get creative and produce a plan on a page that you'll love to share with others.

Here are the steps you might want to take to build this management process.

Step 1: Define content, timelines and interdependencies

Schedule a date once a year to take yourself away and build your plan on a page. In my experience, the best time to do this is during part of the annual budgeting process, so that you can align your plan with forecasts for next year's expenditure. If you need some investment to move your plan forward, these two processes must link. As part of this annual process, after taking yourself away to build the plan, involve your team, share your thoughts and incorporate their input. This helps everyone buy into the plan from the beginning.

Step 2: Assign owners, deliverables and measures

Assign owners and measures for all deliverables in the plan. Don't load all the actions on yourself. Delegate as much as possible.

Step 3: Communicate the entire plan and delegate

Communicate with the wider team and ensure that individuals in your team have objectives that align with the plan, ideally as part of a wider company performance-appraisal process.

Step 4: Measure actual performance against the plan

Each month, publish actual results alongside planned results (with actions required if off course). More on this in management process 3, below.

Step 5: Communicate regularly with everyone

Use your plan in team meetings, one-to-ones, stakeholder meetings and meetings with your manager, and share it with as much of the business as possible.

The overarching goal is to make sure that at any point in time, everyone involved knows the direction of travel, how performance is going in terms of the plan and their specific responsibilities.

Management process 2: Manage stakeholders effectively

In the previous chapter, we explored how to build your stakeholder map. Now, you need a process to embed stakeholder management into your daily routine. Unlike the planning aspect of your role, which tends to link into the business-planning cycle of most organisations' financial calendars, managing your stakeholders is an ongoing activity and should become a regular part of your role as a leader.

The process you set up could look something like this.

Step 1: Prioritise

Consider your map and place each stakeholder in a category – let's use A, B and C as an example. Those in category A are of high importance to you, and you need to connect with them regularly. In this category, include relationships that are either non-existent or badly broken. Those in category B are less important, or you might need to work to improve your relationship with them, regardless of importance. Those in category C are stakeholders of less importance and with whom you have healthy relationships. Think about categories that would work for you and adapt accordingly – there are many ways you could approach this.

Step 2: Improve

Once you've prioritised your stakeholders, decide who will manage each one on an ongoing basis. You and your team members can split this responsibility. Then decide what actions need to be taken and put these into individual schedules. This will normally involve arranging face-to-face meetings or phone calls to set up regular communication channels and understand what both parties need. You might also want to set aside some thinking time to work out why a stakeholder relationship is broken. Is it because you aren't communicating regularly (in which case the preceding action should rectify this)? Or is it a personality clash? Did you get off on the wrong foot and do you need to start again? If so, take the lead on making this happen. Meet (or talk online or on the phone if logistics dictate) with a simple agenda: to get to know the other person better. With an attitude of genuine interest and curiosity, ask them questions to find out about their focus areas, key targets, particular challenges and how they like to work. Over time, try to build a picture of what this person needs to accomplish and if there's a way for you to help. Hopefully, the other person will reciprocate. You can then strengthen the relationship.

It's also important to ensure that in every stakeholder relationship, both parties have complete clarity about what's required from each other. Assume nothing and double-check that you're both on the same page.

Step 3: Review progress and update

On a quarterly basis at least, review your stakeholder map to ensure that you don't need to add or remove anyone and that all the health scores are heading in the right direction. In doing this review, you'll likely catch a deteriorating relationship early, so it doesn't become terminal!

You might be thinking that this is going to take precious time that you haven't got. Yes, it will take time, but the investment will be worth it.

Management process 3: Create a monthly dashboard

This links to your plan on a page, but it's a separate document that monitors progress and keeps your team members accountable. See Appendix 3 or visit www.sandrawebbercoaching.com/books to download an example. I like to set up a traffic-light system similar to the dials at the end of each chapter. The dashboard should reflect all the key deliverables of your plan on a page. You need to decide on some KPIs and assign them a flag. For example, if a KPI is on track, it gets a green flag. If it's slightly behind, it gets an amber flag. And if it's far behind, it gets a red flag. All items with amber or red flags need to be assigned a corrective action. If a KPI is off course intentionally, an explanation needs to be provided.

If you've never set KPIs before, I suggest you find someone who has and get some help. It's not as complicated as it sounds. Here's a simple example of a KPI.

KPI example: Customer-support team

The goal is to respond personally to all customer enquiries (phone, email, online forms) within twenty-four hours of receipt.

Green flag = 100% responses in < 24 hrs

Amber flag = 80% to 99% responses in < 24 hrs

Red flag = 80% responses in < 24 hrs

Don't set too many KPIs. Limit them to critical actions and ensure that they stretch people but are achievable. If the team doesn't buy into them from the beginning, they won't be motivated to achieve them.

Once you've produced a draft of your monthly dashboard, run it past your line manager. If all your KPIs have green flags, your manager and the rest of the business will be delighted with your performance.

Also think of a way to add new projects in your plan on a page to your monthly dashboard so that you can track these as well. Here's an example.

KPI example: Customer relationship management (CRM) system

A new CRM system is being implemented, and several KPIs are required:

- First KPI – Research three possibilities and put forward a business case for recommended option – February XX

- Second KPI – Senior leadership signs off to purchase new CRM system, licensing of software agreed and hardware ordered – March XX

- Third KPI – Devise and sign off implementation plan for new system with owners and timescales – April XX

- Fourth KPI – Implementation plan on track – June XX onwards

- Fifth KPI – New system in place and running well – by the end of August XX

- Sixth KPI – Agree on method for ongoing periodic upgrade of new CRM system with proposals for first upgrade content – by the end of October XX

Once you have a monthly dashboard you're happy with, the final action is to ensure that it's in a format you can carry around, similar to your plan on a page, so that you can use it during meetings with your team, senior managers and stakeholders.

Don't overcomplicate your dashboard. I've worked with organisations whose collection of KPI data becomes a monster process that takes far too long. The dashboard requires too many resources to manage and quickly loses credibility as an effective tool.

Management process 4: Define roles and responsibilities

Performance management isn't a topic we'll go into in this book, but it's something you'll need to master as a leader. If you have an organisation chart showing who reports to whom along with clear job descriptions (JDs), any performance-management issues that arise will be much easier to handle. Some organisations are great at this. They ensure that all roles are clearly defined, to justify any new or replacement positions. If this is the case in your organisation, check that the document used in the hiring process reflects reality and make sure that as part of the induction process, the new recruit is clear about their ultimate role and responsibilities.

If clear JDs aren't in place in your organisation, I recommend creating your own as an Evergreen Executive. Agree on a format with human resources personnel so that everyone in the organisation ends up using the same format.

Example job description format

- Title of role
- Reporting to
- Primary purpose
- Key responsibilities
- KPI ownership

Set up a file that keeps all your JDs in one place with the organisation chart and then review annually, often during performance appraisals, to ensure that everyone's JD reflects reality and there hasn't been any scope creep over the year with business changes.

Management process 5: Maximise people's potential

It may sound counter-intuitive to talk about setting up a process in terms of people, but if you don't systemise how you lead teams of individuals, this aspect of your role can become labour-intensive and frustrating.

With a systematic approach, you can display consistent, fair leadership across your entire team. You might have a small team of direct reports, a large span of control over multiple layers of management or you may be in a role where you're leading a remote or virtual project team that doesn't directly report to you. The principles I outline for this process will work well for you if your team members have solid reporting lines to you. It will be a lot harder if they report to someone else. In these cases, you'll have to build effective partnerships with the line managers responsible for these people. Using the principles of stakeholder management, you can jointly agree on priorities and how to handle underperformance issues in order to lead each person to achieve results.

As an Evergreen Executive responsible for other people, you must strive for excellence throughout your employees' journeys. This involves:

- Recruiting high-calibre people to your team
- Creating an effective and meaningful onboarding/induction process
- Ensuring that each person has complete clarity about their role and what's expected of them, including how they contribute to the overall strategic plan
- Holding regular team meetings

- Getting to know each person in your team

- Holding regular one-to-one discussions with each direct report

- Ensuring people are held accountable for their responsibilities and actions, including their personal development plan

- Conducting meaningful annual appraisals and setting SMART objectives and tailored development plans including a few training activities to aid performance in the person's current role, alongside more developmental ones to complement career ambitions

- Providing regular feedback to ensure motivation stays high and underperformance is addressed in a timely fashion

- Modelling the behaviours of a high performer

- Tailoring your leadership style to different situations

You might be thinking that you haven't got time for all this on top of your job. Well, this is your job as a leader, not a list of nice things to do if you get time – and this is where a lot of leaders go wrong. Optimising your time to work on the above list and delegating tasks to other people are major keys to success.

A high-performing leader's role is to facilitate a team of people to get the required results. The way you do this is via the above list. Developing one of your team members to become your deputy and take on some of your work can also be key. Don't be afraid to let go of the task element of your role. It's part of being an effective leader. You must develop and empower your team members so that you can focus on the seven management processes while others in your team take on more operational tasks.

Let's explore a few areas from the above list where you can gain some quick wins to get started.

Recruit well

Recruitment can be time-consuming and expensive if you don't get it right. Often you'll need to partner with an HR resource. This person should be on your stakeholder map. Hopefully you're now seeing the interconnected approach of this method.

Here's an example recruitment process that you could set up with your HR department:

- Create a clear job description and person spec.

- Design a method of candidate attraction, eg internal notice boards, agency, job-advert websites, LinkedIn, local press.

- Design a method of screening CVs and shortlisting suitable candidates.

- Set up telephone screening – can HR do this for you?

- Hold initial interview and practical test for role – ensure that all interviewers are trained. If there are multiple interviewers, make sure that they're all looking for different things.

- Meet with all interviewers to combine input and filter for next stage.

- Hold final interview with stakeholders, wider team, senior management.

- Provide offer to successful candidate and feedback to unsuccessful candidates.

- Evaluate whether anything could be improved next time.

- The key here is to set up a process that works for you and your organisation so that every time you need to hire, you repeat it.

Ensure induction/onboarding is effective

First impressions really do count. It's terrible when someone who's just joined a team spends their first few days wandering around not knowing what they should be doing, with nowhere to base themselves. It's even worse when no one knows that they just started! I meet a lot of new hires, and the horror stories some of them tell me make me cringe. Within a day, someone can go from being excited to wondering if they made the right decision. Sometimes this ends up setting them off on a route of poor performance and lack of respect for their leader and the organisation.

As an Evergreen Executive, you need to take personal responsibility to make sure that a new hire is correctly brought into your team. Here are some ideas that work well:

- Appoint someone in your team to be the new hire's go-to person. Pick someone who will take pride in this responsibility and display the high-performing attitude and behaviour that you want to create in your team.

- Make sure that you welcome the new hire to your team personally and check in at the end of the first few weeks to see how they're getting on.

- Produce a detailed day-by-day induction time-table – print it out and give it to the new hire.

- Introduce them to the office and get them to spend time with key stakeholders as soon as possible (include this in the induction timetable).

- Check that all logistics are in place, eg desk, computer, HR processes, company car if applicable.

- Ensure that someone talks them through the company's strategy, organisational chart and values so they see where they fit into the big picture.

- Talk them through the job description and encourage questions so they can get clarity.

- If you're going to be away when the new person starts, appoint a deputy to take on your role. As soon as you return, schedule a one-to-one catchup with the new hire to check that all is going to plan – again, encourage questions.

Hold effective team meetings

'You can never over-communicate.' This is a classic leadership mantra, and I agree with it. People often complain to me that communication in their company isn't good and they don't know what's going on. One simple way to ensure that your team are kept informed is to have regular team meetings at a fixed time each month (the fixed time sets a pattern that becomes the norm). You or your deputy should lead these meetings and have a set agenda that allows for a cascade of top-down communication, sharing of information between roles, two-way discussions on specific topics, a way of recognising individuals' positive contributions since the last meeting, a chance to clearly state team priorities and a forum where questions relevant to the whole team can be asked. A well-run meeting that everyone sees as worth attending is a cornerstone of a high-performing team. It's also an opportunity for you to gather feedback you can relay to senior leadership. As leader, it's your responsibility to make sure this meeting happens.

Get to know all team members

Regardless of how skilled you are in your recruitment process, you're never going to really know a person until you've worked alongside them awhile. As an effective leader, spending quality time getting to know your direct reports should be a priority. Meet with them regularly and get to know them and their tasks. When I work with leaders and other clients, I help them identify their personality preferences using a psychometric tool called the Myers Briggs Type Indicator and a couple of charts that get them to consider their underlying values, beliefs and motivations inside and outside of work. Over the years, I've used various tools to get to know people, and I advise each leader to develop their own methodology. It will take a few months to build relationships with individuals so that you can have these genuine discussions, but it will be time well spent. You'll identify how you're similar to this person and how you're different. With this new awareness of each other, both parties should adjust to work more effectively together. That said, as leader, it's your responsibility to adapt and not use the same leadership style with everyone, regardless of the above factors.

Hold regular one-to-one meetings

This process is vital to facilitate the ongoing motivation and alignment of everyone in your team. Regular one-to-one meetings should be prescheduled each month. They can take anything from forty-five to ninety minutes, depending on each individual's maturity and experience in the role and how much support they need from you. Ensure that everyone has a one-to-one with you, even those who are self-sufficient high performers. Poor performers tend to take up a leader's time to the detriment of high performers.

Each one-to-one should be held in a private space, not at a desk in an open-plan office or in a place where either of you could be interrupted. Switch off phones and computers so that the conversation is completely focused on the team member. And make sure the discussion isn't just about to-do lists! This one-to-one should be motivational and meaningful.

If you're running a department and some of your direct reports are also line managers, ensure that they're holding regular one-to-ones with their direct reports. On an ad-hoc basis, check in with the relevant individuals on your team to find out if they're finding these discussions effective.

A standard one-to-one agenda might include the following:

- 'Anything you'd like to discuss?' Ask your direct report this question. After a few meetings, they might start making a list to address. When this happens, it's a good sign that the individual is benefiting from the meetings.

- 'How are you feeling in general?' Ask them to provide a score between 1 and 10, with 1 being low and ten being great, motivated and in control. Try to find out more using questions that start with *what, why, how, where, when* and *what else.*

- Check that their work priorities are in line with your expectations (eg your strategic plan on a page and monthly KPIs and the individual's objectives).

- Follow up on training and development activities that have been agreed or undertaken to ensure that they did happen and that any learnings are embedded into their role.

- Check up on their work-life balance and time management and see if they need your help with prioritisation.

- Check their understanding of any recent company communications and encourage them to ask any questions they might not want to in a bigger group situation.

- Ask if there's any further help or information they need from you as their leader.

- Agree on what actions will be taken as a result of this one-to-one and document them. Follow up on any actions from your previous one-to-one.

Hold individuals accountable

With clear JDs, objectives, development plans and KPIs in place, everyone should know what they need to do, and it's your role to keep them accountable. Review corrective-action plans for any KPIs that are yellow or red and use your monthly one-to-ones to track progress against agreed objectives – this should be routine. If someone is falling behind or absorbing other people's work or if new work is being generated via the business, work with the individuals concerned to reset their to-do lists and offer any support you can.

Also hold people responsible for the actions they commit to at meetings (document this if necessary) and model the correct behaviour by always following through on what you've committed to. Remember, behaviour breeds behaviour. If you have a reputation for never doing what you say you'll do others will think it's okay to do the same. This isn't how a high performer behaves. If you know you can't meet a deadline, communicate a revised one to all concerned with plenty of notice.

Clarify formal objectives and development plans

Every six months, dedicate a good chunk of time within the regular one-to-one or schedule a special meeting to pull out everyone's objectives and development plans and make sure they're still on track, updating where appropriate. Ensure that the individuals involved take responsibility for getting things done but hold them accountable by following up and taking an interest in how they're progressing.

Provide meaningful appraisals

Hopefully your organisation has an annual-review process in which you sit down for between one and two hours with each person in your team to rate their performance, agree on goals for the next year and assess performance in regards to the previous year's goals. This is a chance to give feedback, check motivation and discuss career aspirations, if relevant, and continuous improvement within the current role. Ensure that both you and your team members prepare – the meeting should be a two-way discussion, not feel like a visit to the head teacher's office. If you've never been trained in conducting a meaningful appraisal, this should be part of your development plan. Learn this skill via a training course or watch a few people with good reputations as appraisers conduct them. These appraisals should be worthwhile conversations that are motivating for both parties, not a box-ticking exercise done for the sake of the HR department.

Set SMART objectives

S: State specifically what you want the person to do and what 'good' looks like.

M: Set a measurement so you know whether the objective has been met. Set an outcome.

A: Make sure the objective is achievable.

R: Make sure it's relevant – why does it need to be done?

T: Clarify the time in which it needs to be completed.[15]

If your organisation doesn't have a formal goal-setting process, set up a similar one yourself. There are many types of appraisal forms, from simplistic, concise ones to lengthy options. I prefer the shorter versions, based on my personality type. If you want to know how to devise your own, drop me an email using the contact details at the end of this book.

Provide regular feedback

There's nothing more demotivating than working in an environment where you never hear anything, good or bad, from your leader. Some personalities need more feedback than others, but an Evergreen Executive makes it a priority to give regular feedback, both positive and corrective, to all team members.

15 GT Doran, 'Theres a S.M.A.R.T way to Write Managements Goals and Objectives', *Management Review (AMA Forum)*, November 1981, https://community.mis.temple.edu/mis0855002fall2015/files/2015/10/S.M.A.R.T-Way-Management-Review.pdf, accessed 3 April 2020.

Until this becomes a habit, you may need something (eg a table) to remind you to look out for situations where you can give meaningful feedback. For example, if a team member received positive client feedback, acknowledge how great this is. If a member made an impactful presentation to another team, let them know how powerful it was. If a member worked hard to improve a process or set up a new system, acknowledge their contribution. Also, if someone made a mistake, let them know and work with them so they understand the corrective action.

Deliver all feedback with the genuine intent of helping the recipient develop their skill set and improve their performance.

Proactively manage performance issues

As soon as an individual in your team starts to underperform, let them know that they're off track. Don't wait until the annual-performance appraisal. It's much easier to nip things in the bud. The reason why new hires have a probation period is so you can assess whether they can do the job they've been hired for and so they can work out whether the job is for them.

Use these initial few months to give feedback, as discussed, and ensure the person is set up for success.

If any existing team member is performing below the required standards, use the regular one-to-ones to ensure that they fully understand what they need to do and that they have sufficient training. Make sure they're receiving feedback both when they're doing the right thing and when they're not.

Initially, it's your responsibility as their leader to make sure that they perform the job correctly. Only if a solid plan of action to get the person back on track fails should you turn to human resources expertise and explore what actions to take if the person isn't capable of doing the job in question. This should be a last resort. There may be a more suitable role that the person could be moved to.

Link each person into your plan

This is an important piece of the organisational masterplan, and it's often missed. You need to illustrate to each of your team members how they contribute to your overall strategic plan on a page. Some roles can seem far removed from top-level company discussions, and it's your job as leader of a high-performing team to regularly remind everyone where they fit in and why their jobs make a difference.

My first leadership role within Hewlett Packard was a supervisory position in the Bristol factory's accounts-payable department. The factory was going through a period of rapid growth, and the invoice-processing team had got out of control, hence the need for my role. The spotlight was on the team for the wrong reasons; it had just failed an internal audit, and suppliers to the factory weren't getting paid on time, so production could be put on hold at any minute. I like a challenge, but within a few weeks of starting in the role, I realised the challenge was bigger than I'd expected. The team of five permanent employees were fed up. They were working crazy hours to keep their heads above water alongside temporary workers who'd been brought in to help them get things back under control.

At the end of my first month in the position, I pulled the team together, and we took a whole day to put an action plan together. I still remember this day clearly. I was standing at the front of the room with a flip chart trying to motivate a tired workforce. At the end of the session, I made sure everyone in the team, including all the temporary staff and me, walked away with specific action items. That session was a turning point, as everyone saw they had a personal role to play in the improvement plan. It took six months of hard work, but we cleared the backlog, improved our day-to-day operating processes to get back in control and passed both internal and external audits successfully. The team was back in the spotlight, and this time for the right reasons. The key was everyone knowing what role they played in the plan.

Be a positive role model

This is so important for many reasons, as we'll discuss in depth later in the book. It bears repeating: behaviour breeds behaviour. If your team members see you behaving in a certain way, they'll likely mirror this, assuming it's the standard.

Two interrelated examples that come up in relation to this are work-life balance and time management. It's difficult to have fruitful discussions with your team about either of these topics if you spend crazy hours in the office, work weekends, don't take holidays, miss deadlines or don't complete the actions you say you're going to. You won't come across as credible. It's also difficult to motivate others when you come across as unmotivated.

As an Evergreen Executive, you're in the spotlight. This can be difficult. You have to be an example of excellence most of the time. We're all allowed an off day – no one is perfect. But 95% of the time, you must show what 'good' looks like to inspire others to do the same. You are leading by example every day.

Tailor your leadership style

Finally, it's important to tailor your approach to each team member so that you can help them maximise their potential, from the time you first become their leader to the time either you or they move on. Consider the person's personality preferences, what motivates them, their experience and their capability in the role. Situational leadership is a popular model that's been around for years and is still valid.[16]

Management process 6: Optimise your time

As illustrated in the previous process, being an exceptional leader involves a lot. This is why, when I meet one, I have great admiration for them. They might

---

16 Business Balls, 'Situational Leadership Model – Hersey and Blanchard', www.businessballs.com/leadership-models/situational-leadership-model-hersey-and-blanchard, accessed 3 April 2020.

make it look easy but it isn't. And a lot of 'making it look easy' comes down to time management.

You might have multiple stakeholders vying for your time and endless meetings to attend. Weeks might go by where you don't do anything in management process 5; meanwhile, your personal to-do list grows. On top of this, there might be pressure in your home life, or you might feel resentful that you don't have time to spend on the well-being activities covered in the first part of this book.

If this is the case, you need to implement an exceptional time-management method. This will involve delegating to others and learning to say no to some things. If this is a natural strength, great. If not, you might find it useful to do these things:

- Refer to your plan on a page to remind yourself where you should be spending your time
- Familiarise yourself with Stephen Covey's four-box model[17]

---

17   Covey, *The 7 Habits of Highly Effective People*.

- Identify your personal time-stealing habits (eg email, internet, rescuing people, meetings, poor performers)

One resource that we all have is twenty-four hours. What you have a choice about is how you use those hours.

BRETT　　　　　　　*Case Study*

In prior roles, Brett had thought that time management was one of his strengths. Yet in his current role, he had an extremely long to-do list that never seemed to get shorter. He also had a reputation for turning up late to meetings, and his work-life balance was non-existent – his home life and his health were suffering.

It took a couple of coaching sessions for Brett to realise that his natural time-management skills were being impacted by his direct manager, who didn't excel in this area. The company's chaotic culture wasn't helping either. In his previous roles, Brett had worked for structured, efficient leaders, and the industries were, by nature, process and timetable driven.

Once he understood this, Brett thought back to his old methods that had worked and decided to use them even though his managers and peers weren't used to operating in such a disciplined way. This is a common situation – even high performers can get sucked into a way of working that's the norm but doesn't serve them.

Over the course of a few weeks, Brett reverted to his old habit of carrying with him at all times an A4 daybook, which he took to all meetings. Afterwards, he'd add any actions assigned to him to his master to-do list. Then, he'd determine whether he could delegate any actions. If so, he'd delegate immediately or note the action under the relevant person's name so he could discuss it with them in their next one-to-one. He booked monthly one-to-ones in advance with all his direct reports and arranged a monthly meeting for himself with his line manager.

He began to question whether he could send another team member to certain meetings he was asked to attend, and he set aside fifteen minutes prior to each meeting he did attend to allow transit time across the site. At the end of each day, he spent half an hour creating his to-do list for the next working day, and he'd work from home on one day every other week, so he'd have fewer interruptions and could have some quality thinking time. He also made sure he left the office on time at least two days per week.

These little actions helped him regain control. It didn't matter if no one else in the company operated this way because he felt much better.

It's a challenge for an Evergreen Executive to keep their personal standards high if the people around them aren't operating in a similar way, but it's important to maintain your standards of self-management. Remember, you're a role model for others. And sometimes, you might have to lead the way across an entire organisation.

Management process 7: Stay current

The wider your span of control becomes or the more responsibilities you get, the harder it is to make time for your own work and development. But it's important to practise what you preach to your team members. You must stay up to date on company-wide information as well as industry or professional knowledge. It's a key responsibility.

Sometimes your professional role may demand that you spend time on your own development. You might need to submit proof that you've undertaken a specific number of continuous-professional-development hours. As an accountant I was required to do this, and now as a professional coach, every three years I need to complete a comprehensive mentoring, observation, training and client-work process to retain my membership in the federation I'm part of. Many of my clients, from doctors to lawyers to project managers, must undertake similar work to comply with their relevant institutes and professional bodies. Although we might complain about having to comply with these requirements, and although they can be costly in terms of time and fees, it's kind of nice when we're forced to do it. It's more difficult to focus on professional development if you don't have an external professional requirement.

One leader I worked with kept a 'reading tray' on their desk. It included industry articles, publications recommended by other colleagues, a list of TED talks they wanted to check out and documents produced by stakeholders, competitors, suppliers and customers. They scheduled a Friday-afternoon reading session once a month. And they scheduled a self-development day (which would involve either self-study at home or a workshop, conference or webinar) once a quarter. They also linked their own professional development into their stakeholder-management system and set up meetings with knowledgeable people, using the time to get a briefing from them in their area of expertise. In the spirit of give and take, this leader also held briefings at lunchtime for anyone interested in learning about their specialism within the industry. Not only did this help others develop, but it also raised the leader's profile across the organisation as an expert in their field.

If you're in danger of neglecting your self-development, you might want to work with a mentor or coach who can hold you accountable for this. And ensure that it's specifically mentioned in your own training and development plan. Remember, 'keep growing' is in the subtitle of this book!

The systems element of professional excellence might seem like a lot to consider, but investing time in the processes outlined in this chapter means that they'll become embedded in your everyday activities and make your role a lot easier in the long run.

Below is a summary of how all seven systems interrelate.

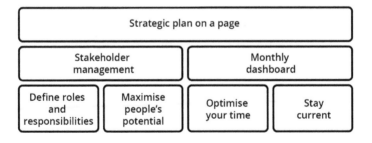

Management systems summary

Reflection questions

- Can you see the benefit of setting up your role as a leader in such a systematic way?

- Do you do any of these things already? Perhaps you just need to be consistent or fine-tune?

- Is there anything happening soon that you could use as a catalyst to set up a system? Perhaps you need to hire someone. If so, make sure you have a clear job description and induction process in your model.

- Have you used any of these processes in a prior role? Can you repeat previous actions?

- Do any other leaders work in a similar way to you? Could you use the same templates?

- Do you have a quarterly process for your own professional improvement, including continuing professional development for your specific functional skills?

- Who could keep you accountable for setting these systems up?

Suggested next steps

- Schedule time to create the processes listed in this chapter.

- Allow yourself time to set up these processes properly (eg six to twelve months) because once they're in place, they'll last a lifetime. This stuff doesn't change.

Where are you starting from?

Using the dial below, rate yourself in this area today.

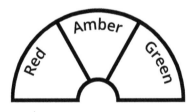

Systems

- Green zone – in good shape

- Amber zone – work to be done

- Red zone – immediate action required

CHAPTER 8

Status

This section is about you. How you show up in the world is important professionally and personally because it will directly impact your credibility as a high-performing leader. I prefer to think of what's often called personal branding as the footprint you leave behind whenever you interact with people or deliver results.

Is this something that you've thought about before now? If you've been working for organisations that encourage regular 360-degree feedback or ask you to gather input from others before workshops or as part of your annual appraisal, you may have an idea of how others view you. If you haven't, you're in new territory.

Strong leaders are consistent, not only in their actions but also in their moods. I've worked with unpredictable people and within the first hour of the working day could determine whether it was going to be a good day or a bad one!

Self-awareness is vital in personal development. If, at this stage, you have no idea what people think about you, you must take action to find out so that you know what you do well (and need to continue doing) as well as what isn't working in your favour (and needs more work as far as professional credibility is concerned).

Random action point: Look at your stakeholder map and pick out five to ten people with different ratings in terms of relationship health. Ask these people: 'What are three of my strengths? What are three areas I could improve in?'

An Evergreen Executive stands apart from others in that they're memorable for all the right reasons, which will be explored in this chapter. Either they have these traits naturally or, more commonly, they've developed them over many years.

Traits of an Evergreen Executive

Reliable

You need to be seen as someone who can be relied upon to do what you say you're going to do within an agreed timescale – someone who doesn't need to be chased or reminded because people know that you'll always do what you've said you would. If there's any chance that you might not meet a deadline, let people know. If you need further information to complete your actions, get it; don't use this as an excuse to delay completion.

Results and outcome driven

Always get clarity on what deliverables are needed – this should be your standard mode of operation. Strive to create a full picture in your mind of what others expect of you. Where the outcomes are unclear, keep asking questions to get clarity, and if you still don't get it, formulate an idea of what you think the result should be and put this forward to check if it's right or wrong.

Able to embrace change

One thing is certain – things will always change. And others will note your attitude towards any changes, good or bad. Some people resist change, but as a high-performing leader, you can't. You're responsible for leading others through any changes as well as for handling your own reaction. You'll need to develop the skills to take people quickly through the Change Curve[18] so that performance levels and results aren't adversely affected by organisational-system, process or personnel changes. If this is an area you need to work on, familiarise yourself with the five stages of the Change Curve to learn more about how often emotional reactions to change can impact performance.

Evergreen Executives thrive in times of change because they're a chance to demonstrate leadership versatility. They can adapt personally and lead their teams. They can create new plans, develop new systems and improve processes.

18 E Kübler-Ross, *Death and Dying* (Scribner, 1969; reprinted Simon & Schuster, 2014).

High energy/fun to work with/positive

These phrases tell you how you need to be 95% of the time! In *Own It*, I categorised people into three weather types – Dark Storms, Cloudy Skies and Rays of Sunshine.[19] The Evergreen Executive is a Ray of Sunshine. They are the leader everyone wants to work for and with. If you're an Evergreen Executive, people will look forward to attending your meetings, as your energy is infectious and they'll feel better after working with you. Even in the most challenging of business situations, you're fun to work with and have a positive influence on those around you.

Being one of these leaders takes skill and hard work underpinned by the habits and techniques explored in the first part of this book. If any of your personal energy dials are in the amber or red zones, that's where developmental work is needed. Doing this work will massively impact your professional footprint.

Find a leader in your organisation who is a Ray of Sunshine and watch and learn from them. Get them to mentor you. Spend as much time with them as you can.

---

19 S Webber, *Own It: Regain control and live life on your terms* (Rethink Press, 2016).

Highly self-aware

Becoming self-aware is an ongoing project. Gain knowledge of yourself by attending workshops, doing self-study and mentoring or coaching others. Feedback should be gratefully received and, if not offered, proactively sought out. We all have strengths and areas that need developing, and those who have done the work to learn these things know themselves well and are comfortable in their own skin. They give off an authentic energy that enhances their professional and personal status. Someone who's comfortable admitting both their positive and negative character traits in a neutral way will come across as real and easy to work with. These people aren't pretending to be something they're not. An Evergreen Executive is happy being themselves. It's inspiring to others.

One trait that enhances a person's professional status is the ability to know if they're not the right person to take on a task and to state this and walk away rather than try to muddle their way through it. You'll achieve the best results all around if you have the confidence to say you aren't the best person to take on a responsibility but know someone in your network you can recommend. This is a win-win situation: you strengthen your credibility and give back to your network.

Well connected

Working in partnership with others is the norm in business. We acknowledge that we all have strengths and areas of development, so what better way to plug the skills and behaviour gaps than by working with others who have these particular skills and behaviours?

Building a powerful network is an art. Approach it with a give-and-take attitude. Make it your aim to enjoy connecting with people even if there's no obvious or immediate benefit to you. People can create negative reputations for themselves if they're always taking from people or going into relationships with a personal motive, suspicious of other people's motives. You need to develop the skill of being able to routinely add to your network people who operate to the standards outlined in this book and stay in contact with them. Like attracts like, and it you have high standards and show up as a Ray of Sunshine professionally and personally, others like you will proactively build relationships with you and want to stay connected with you.

It's also rewarding to put two people in contact with each other and have both parties thank you many years later because the resulting relationship was so successful. This is part of creating a strong network.

The network you create around you doesn't have to be huge, but it must have high-quality people.

Committed to continually improving and learning

Evergreen Executives know that a process or an individual's performance can be continually improved. They're always looking to see how things could be more efficient, how to enhance a customer or employee experience and how to improve all the KPIs in their area. When striving to exceed expectations and delight stakeholders, you need to constantly encourage yourself and your team to develop.

Many years ago, I ran a leadership programme for a company. As part of an icebreaker at the beginning of day one, I asked each of the fifteen managers to rate themselves as a leader between 1 and 10, 1 being inexperienced with a lot to learn and 10 being experienced and knowing everything. One person rated themselves as a 10, and I couldn't help but think that I could never do that. Even though I've done this type of work for over thirty years, I'm still learning.

The world of work changes all the time, and to keep your professional status high, you also have to evolve.

Mindful of boundaries

Working on your personal brand is a full-time job. If you want to be an Evergreen Executive, you can never get complacent about this aspect of your professional life. It takes a lot of hard work to create an exceptional brand and consistency to maintain it – and it can be ruined quickly.

Early in my professional life, I worked for a large corporation whose culture was 'work hard and play hard'. I observed people who maintained their professional brand at all times and those who diluted or ruined it by not respecting certain professional boundaries. In the fun, social part of corporate life, it's easy to let your guard down. As the drinks flow at work social events, you often see a different side to your colleagues, and they also see a different side to you. Alcohol enables us to relax and speak more freely, but I've witnessed a few too many inappropriate conversations between drunk employees and less drunk or completely sober senior managers. That's not to say the opposite doesn't happen – it does, and the consequences are equally embarrassing and can result in career suicide.

One mentor of mine would attend these occasions but would have only one drink and leave or stick to soft drinks all night and drive. She loved to drink more freely but saved this for when she was socialising without colleagues.

Another important boundary is confidentiality. If you're easy to approach and talk to (both are traits of an Evergreen Executive), it's likely that a lot of people will confide in you and you'll know a lot of information. Similarly, if you work in human resources or on a strategic leadership team, you'll be privy to a lot of confidential information. It's vital that you don't share such information with the wrong people. The higher you progress within an organisation, the more often you'll hear about projects or major decisions before they're widely communicated. Some people will try to get this information from you, believing that information is power. Respecting this confidentiality boundary is non-negotiable.

Supportive of others' development

To leave behind a positive professional footprint, you need to be a leader who's willing to help others progress and share any experiences or expertise that could be useful. When you display professional excellence, others will want to know how you do it, and there's great satisfaction in seeing others develop as a result of your guidance.

Acting as a formal or informal mentor to others comes with the territory of being a high performer, but it's important to establish professional boundaries here as well. Be careful not to take on too many mentees at any one time – you could end up jeopardising your own performance. Also make sure that your mentees don't become too dependent on you. In the long term, your role as a good mentor is to enable others to become self-sufficient. For this reason, if someone asks you to act as their mentor, it's important to agree to the contract terms of this working relationship up front. The mentee should drive the logistical arrangements.

Here are some things you might want to include in an informal contract:

- What does the mentee want your help with? (Establish from this information whether you're the right mentor for them. Are you proficient in the skills they need help with? Have you walked the path they want to walk? If you aren't the right person, you may know someone in your network who's better placed than you, and you could initiate an introduction.)

- How often will you meet, and how long will each meeting be?

- Will you offer support between sessions?

- How long will the mentoring last? (Based on my experience, meeting monthly over a period of six to eight months works well.)

Value coaching/mentoring

Most high performers and successful individuals, even those with senior roles in huge organisations, have their own coach or mentor because they've realised the value of this. Check out the TED talk clip 'Everyone Needs a Coach' with Bill Gates and Eric Schmidt on YouTube.[20] It's worth a watch.

It can be lonely at the top of an organisation, or if you're responsible for a lot of people or huge budgets. Sometimes it might feel as if there's no one to go to for support. It's vital to have your own confidential support system. You need a safe space to talk things through and get personal feedback from someone with no other agenda than to help you be successful. Since you need to be encouraging your direct reports to develop themselves continually, it's important that you act as a role model in this regard.

When someone demonstrates all the traits and behaviours listed in this chapter, they stand out from the crowd. Their names often come up in conversation, and few people at any level in the organisation have a bad word to say about them. They achieve a lot. They work hard but are positive and make time for people. They're happy to mentor others but often have a waiting list, as they can take on only a

---

20 B Gates and E Schmidt, 'Everyone Needs a Coach' [YouTube video], 21 February 2017, www.youtube.com/watch?v=8R1pHd4niLl, accessed 03 April 2020. See also www.ted.com for more TED talks.

couple of people at a time. Other senior managers seek their input, and they're often specifically asked to be part of strategically important projects. They manage their time effectively, so they also have a life outside of work, which is hugely inspiring. They have a down-to-earth, genuine energy, and they're able to communicate well at all levels and deliver inspiring presentations.

I recently worked as an executive coach for a large organisation, and two people quickly became visible to me. After I'd had a couple of meetings with them and had worked within the company for a few months, it was evident that these two leaders had developed the traits covered in this book. What stood out first, though, was how easy they were to work with and their positive attitudes despite the real problems in the business and the huge dissatisfaction radiating across the sites. These two leaders remained stead-fast, continuing the basic processes and modes of operation that they knew worked. Whenever I met them in the corridors, they always had time to talk, even when the pressure was on. Their well-being was a top priority, and they kept up monthly one-to-one meetings with their direct reports despite their extraordinary workload. They had embedded the

Evergreen Executive way of working so well that the tougher the business climate became, the brighter they shone.

In a nutshell, your personal footprint should be something that others admire. Be known for all the right reasons. Walk the talk in an authentic way, both in terms of the results that you deliver and how you go about your professional life and your personal one.

Reflection questions

- Have you got enough feedback to assess your current status?

- When did you last work with a mentor or coach?

Suggested next steps

- Rate yourself against the traits listed in this chapter.

- Get current feedback from a wide variety of people to inform your self-assessment.

- Pick three things that you can work on to improve your footprint.

Where are you starting from?

Using the dial below, rate yourself in this area today.

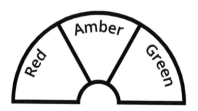

Status

- Green zone – in good shape
- Amber zone – work to be done
- Red zone – immediate action required

CHAPTER 9

Building Your Action Plan

This is when the rubber hits the road!

How many books have you read and put back on the shelf, never to be picked up again? I've designed this book to minimise the chances of this happening – I want it to be something you carry around and use so much that eventually it looks well worn. Over time, all the habits and processes should become embedded, so you'll use it less, but it might become a useful training tool for any leaders that report to you or anyone you mentor. Make notes in a journal or an online document about anything that you need to work on and embed. You can also print off the example templates at www.sandrawebbercoaching.com/books and either use them as they are or tweak and personalise.

What does the summary version of your dashboard look like? Now that you've worked through each chapter, put all the dial information together on the dashboard below.

Your summary dashboard

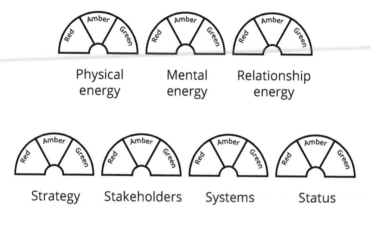

Summary dashboard

This should give you a foundation on which you can devise an improvement plan.

How you go about creating a plan to improve your performance as a leader is entirely up to you. If you need an idea, see the example improvement plan in Appendix 4. There's a strong argument for working on your personal energy first. You'll feel a sense of well-being that will allow you to tackle more systematic work. Conversely, if you become more formulaic in the professional side of your life, this could increase your sense of well-being and complement the actions you take to increase your personal energy.

The worst possible outcome is taking no action. Where you start doesn't matter. All the dials need to turn to the green zone over time if you want to operate as an Evergreen Executive.

On the subject of time, how much time do you want to set aside to make significant improvements to your dashboard? Set yourself a SMART goal (see management process 5).

Here's an example:

> To undertake another self-assessment exercise in six months' time [insert exact date] and have no dials in the red zone. To repeat the exercise in twelve months' time [insert exact date] and have no dials in the red or amber zone.

Your SMART goal is entirely your creation – you need to drive the action.

You might choose to start where you're currently experiencing the most pain, as this can really drive action. Another strategy is to consider where you can make some instant changes and, in business speak, 'pick some low-hanging fruit', as seeing quick progress is also motivating.

If, for example, the organisation you're working for is about to start a new planning cycle, it might make sense for you to start with the strategy session and create your plan on a page.

No rights or wrongs! The aim is to get you operating with dials in the green zone all the time!

I've worked with many people over the last thirty years, and certain patterns emerge when it comes to taking action. Let's look at a few now.

Energetic start before fizzling out

Some people get to work straight away. They behave like a fire that's just been lit and decide they're going to act on all fronts with a scattergun approach. This type of person would look at the dashboard and want to take enthusiastic action on every dial at the same time, believing that they could quickly get all the dials into the green zone.

Initially, this is inspiring to see. It appears as if all the person needed was some encouragement and information on what to do. The problem is that this level of action and intensity over a wide range of tasks, behavioural changes, process setups and habit formation is unsustainable. A lot of the up-front activity eventually decreases and then fades out before any long-term changes are made. People who take this approach often find their dials in the exact same position in a year's time.

Then there's the opposite type of person.

More research needed

Even after reading the ideas in this book and assessing their current performance in terms of personal energy and professional excellence, this type of person still won't be ready to commit. What they need is more reassurance that this is right for them, so they'll either gather information that verifies or invalidates what they've just read or talk to a few people to get their input. This person might spend hours in the endless Google-search arena only to find many more ideas and approaches that they could implement.

Don't get me wrong – there's a lot of great information out there, and as a learning and development addict myself, I love the inspiration I get from listening to, watching or reading about others in the fields of personal development, leadership and living life to the fullest. The problem with this approach is that you can gather information endlessly, and the more you gather, the more confusing things can become. Eventually, this person might stop taking action altogether because they're afraid they might be heading down the wrong path.

Then there are...

Excuses, excuses

Of all the types of people, the person who makes excuses is the one that I find most frustrating to work with. Some leaders fall into the trap of blaming their underperformance on something or someone else and don't take responsibility. Common phrases I hear are 'my manager isn't good', 'my team is completely demotivated' and 'I'm so busy that I haven't got time to do this'.

These people have taken on the victim role and must realise that no one can help them except themselves. I'm hoping that you're not in this category, as you're reading this book, but if you have anyone in your team like this, it's your job to challenge them to take responsibility for improving their performance, regardless of any barriers they see. Encourage them to work on things over which they have control and to not spend time worrying about things they can't control. Once more: behaviour breeds behaviour. If people see you changing, behaving differently physically and mentally, improving your health and getting results, some of them, though not all, will become curious. When they show an interest, share some of the changes you've made and they may be inspired to do the same. Someone has to lead the way, so why can't you?

And then there's this approach...

Pragmatically attacking pain points

Initially, this approach looks good because some things will get done quickly. The person taking this approach will focus on the area that's causing them the most pain. For example, to increase their personal energy, they might start eating healthy lunches and take a daily walk on the office grounds. And to increase their professional excellence, they might introduce effective regular team meetings. These are good things.

The long-term issue with this approach is that it's piecemeal. It will turn a couple of the dials in the right direction, but only a couple. What happens to the other dials? At best, they're going to stay the same, and at worst, they could move the opposite way.

The approach that's recommended, and one I've seen work best is...

Building a structured action plan to embed new habits

Becoming an Evergreen Executive and consistently leading like one doesn't happen overnight. Action can be taken immediately, though, primarily in the form of a mindset shift – you need to accept that you are embarking on a twelve- to eighteen-month-long systematic improvement plan that will inevitably have its ups and downs. But you'll have the personal commitment and support structure to ensure that you drive your action plan through in its entirety until it becomes a way of life for you as a high-performing leader.

MAGGIE   *Case Study*

Maggie, an office manager within the IT industry, is the perfect example of this approach. When we first met, she was about to fall into the victim mindset. She wondered if she needed a complete career change because she hated her role. This dislike for her job, and the fact that she'd felt like this for a long time, had started to translate into poor performance, and she was worried about being put in the first stage of the in-house disciplinary process because she'd failed to meet her personal objectives. Through initial discussions, it became clear that Maggie didn't really want to leave the company but didn't know how to turn her situation around.

Maggie needed to do a lot of work on her dashboard, and she went away to think about what she could do. Given that she'd been close to the victim mindset, I was delighted when she came into our third session beaming. With her, she had a file she'd created, and it was split into seven colour-coded sections. At the front was her master plan with ideas for her targets for each dial and timescales attached, along with key milestones at specific points. I love a good plan, and this one was exceptional. It followed a structure similar to a plan on a page. It was powerful, inspirational and immediately elevated the professional impression she left with me.

Maggie left a very different footprint on session three, compared to the one she left on our first session. The other thing I noticed was how she lit up when she talked me through her plan and how willing she was to amend and update her thinking as she gathered more input and clarity regarding what needed to be done. Her plan was also realistic. It wasn't a quick-fix approach – in fact, according to her plan, it was going to take two years to get all her dials into the green zone! Some people might have been put off by the scale of this plan and the long timescale, but this didn't faze her. She was excited about the challenge and the anticipated sense of satisfaction that she'd get when it all came to fruition.

I continued to meet with Maggie over the next six months. She implemented her plan and it evolved over time to incorporate changes in her team, strategic changes within the company and an expansion of her role. Maggie always brought her file to our sessions. She'd created an online version as a backup and also so she could share it with her line manager, who'd become interested in her approach after noticing a change in her energy levels and her more positive attitude. Within these six months, Maggie got off the 'below job standard' radar and was ranked at the high end of acceptable. Colleagues had noticed her new approach, and she was starting to impact other areas of the business. She was still reporting to the same line manager, whom she'd complained a lot about in her first session. But her mindset had changed completely in that she was committed to taking ownership of her area of responsibility and doing the best she possibly could.

At each of our sessions, we looked in detail at how her professional excellence improvement plan was going, and we spent time discussing the personal energy dials. Maggie gradually began to shift these from red and amber to green by incorporating better eating habits, going to the gym before work and surrounding herself with like-minded people inside and outside of work. She also started using her long commute to listen to inspiring podcasts and no longer begrudged her time in the car. One breakthrough change she made was gaining permission to work from home every other Friday. This allowed her to update her overall project plan and get valuable thinking time away from the office to work out strategies for the hardest elements of her role.

Over the first year, we had a few check-in sessions, during which she'd update me on her master plan. There were ups and downs in the process, as life threw in a few curveballs and a couple of unforeseeable challenges occurred at work, one of them being a complete office relocation that they asked her to lead. Whenever Maggie was having a particularly rough time, she rang me or her mentor. This gave her the opportunity to talk things through in a confidential safe space, after which she could work out what to do next.

Then I didn't hear from Maggie for a while, but I wasn't worried because I knew she'd developed the ability to look after herself and had a good support system to call on if required. She'd become a great, credible leader within that first year and was enjoying her role again.

Two years after we first met, she emailed me about a company awards dinner and said she'd won an award for outstanding leadership contribution. She was shocked and delighted. She'd also been promoted to head of operations and was enjoying her broader remit. In taking on this new role a couple of months prior, she'd repeated the process that she'd used before, created a new strategic plan and mentored a couple of members within her existing team to take on supervisory roles. As part of the mentoring, she'd trained them in the importance of having a master plan, setting up key management systems to support her own, satisfying all their key stakeholders and ensuring that they left professional footprints they could be proud of inside and outside of the organisation. Her mental turnaround and progress were amazing to see, and she had a queue of people wanting to be mentored by her.

In addition to all her professional progress, she'd also moved house, lost a stone in weight and got herself a place in the London Marathon.

Maggie's story shows that playing the long game pays off if you want to make changes that eventually become your standard way of living and leading. The long game can be years rather than months, and changes aren't easily embedded in weeks, so it's the tortoise's approach rather than the hare's that's required here!

Reflection questions

- How have you been taking action?
- What might you need to do differently to move towards the structured-action-over-time methodology?

Suggested next steps

- Devise your own improvement plan.
- Find someone to hold you accountable for it and build in review dates.
- Execute it, adapt it, continue taking action and enjoy the journey professionally and personally.

Wrapping Up

So that's it! We've covered a lot in this book, and as I've said throughout, being an Evergreen Executive leader isn't easy, especially at the beginning.

But it's worth developing yourself in this way.

In doing so, you'll keep growing throughout your career. It's rewarding on many levels. You can work on interesting things with inspiring people while helping others make the same journey.

I hope you'll take whatever actions are right for you.

The role of a leader is important, and it can be rewarding both personally and professionally. Enjoy the journey!

Appendices

Appendix 1: Strategic plan on a page

Created by: _____ Last updated: _____

Department: _____

Vision statement:

_____

_____

Year 1 key goals

    1.

    2.

    3.

Year 2/3 key goals

    1.

    2.

    3.

Operational process	Owner	SMART goals	Notes
Example: Month-end financial accounts	F. Manager	To produce month-end accounts and present to the Senior Leadership Team by seventh work day of each month	
Example: Monthly team meetings	A. Leader	Full team meetings to be held in the third week of every month	All actions to be circulated within 24 hours
Process 3			
Process 4			
Process 5			
Key projects	Owner	SMART goals	Notes
Example: To implement a fully automated expenses system across all departments	E. Manager	A fully functioning expenses system with all employees fully trained in how to use it by November XXXX	
Project 2			
Project 3			

Appendix 2: Stakeholder mapping and health check

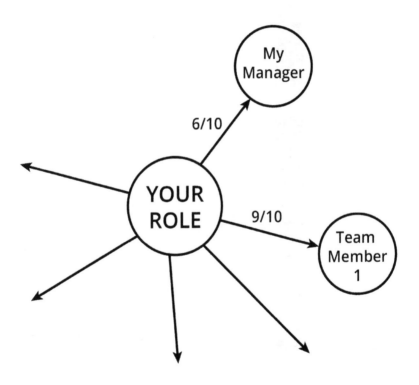

Appendix 3: Monthly dashboard

Created by: _____

Last updated: _____

Department: _____

Process	Owner	Flag Status	Jan	Feb	Mar	April	May	June	July	Aug	Sept	Oct	Nov	Dec
Production of final month-end accounts	A.n. Other	Green < workday 7 Amber workday 8–9 Red workday 9	Red	Red	Amber									
Monthly 1-1s	T. Leader	Green < all member have 1-1 Amber 1–2 dont have 1-1s Red. 3+ don't have 1-1s	Amber	Green	Green									

New expense system	J. Brown	Green < project plan 100% on target Amber 1–3 missed Red > 3 missed											

Appendix 4: Personal improvement plan

Created by: _____   Last updated: _____

EE dial area	Quick-win action (now!)	6-month action steps	12-month goal	Notes
Physical energy				
Mental energy				
Relationship energy				
Strategy				
Stakeholders				
Systems				
Status				
Notes				

Additional Resources

Books

Freer A, *Eat, Nourish, Glow: 10 easy steps for losing weight, looking younger and feeling healthier* (Thorsons, 2015)

Peters S, *The Chimp Paradox: The acclaimed mind management programme to help you achieve success, confidence and happiness* (Vermilion, 2012)

Priestley D, *Key Person of Influence: The five-step method to become one of the most highly valued and highly paid people in your industry* (Rethink Press, 2014)

Roth B, *Strength in Stillness: The power of transcendental meditation* (Simon & Schuster, 2018)

Wilson J, *Adrenal Fatigue: The 21st century stress syndrome* (Smart Publications, 2002)

Podcasts

Chatterjee R, *Feel Better, Live More,* https://drchatterjee.com/blog/category/podcast

Howes L, *The School of Greatness*, https://lewishowes.com/sogpodcast

Millburn JR and Nicodemus R, *The Minimalists,* www.theminimalists.com/podcast

Roll R, *The Rich Roll Podcast,* www.richroll.com/category/podcast

Webber S, *The Career Tree (formerly Own It)* https://ownitpodcasts.wordpress.com

Winfrey O, *Supersoul Conversations,* www.oprah.com/app/supersoul-sunday-full-episodes.html

Acknowledgements

I am grateful to all those people who have supported my writing this book and helped me improve both the content and structure over many months. In particular I would like to thank Bonnie, Dave, Gill and Laura, who saw the very raw version of the manuscript.

My thanks again to the Rethink Press team, especially Lucy and Joe, who make the whole book-writing process easy and fun!

The Author

Sandra is a professional coach who works with both businesses and private clients primarily in the UK and Europe. She specialises in executive coaching, helping leaders improve their own performance and create high-performing teams. In addition, she also works with individuals as a career coach and in a personal development capacity.

She is co-director of The Kudos Group, a training and development company that has supported a huge variety of business clients for over twenty years. The team members provide outsourced training and development support, training programmes and strategic HR services.

Sandra is extremely pragmatic and outcome driven in her approach as a coach. She takes a genuine interest in each client as they work towards their individual professional and personal goals.

She started her career in the beauty industry before transitioning into administration and finance roles. She qualified as a chartered management accountant while working full time as a finance manager. She spent seventeen years working for Hewlett Packard Ltd in their finance, quality and human resources department before leaving corporate life in July 2000.

Less than two months after leaving Hewlett Packard, Sandra set up Kudos Events Ltd with a business partner and spent two years running conferences, seminars and charity events before refocusing Kudos into becoming the training and development company that it still is today with an impressive client list that's still expanding.

Outside of work, Sandra juggles her passion for healthy living and well-being with a large blended family currently made up of her partner, five grown-up children and five grandchildren ranging in age from two to seventeen. Sandra and her partner regularly spend time living and working in Palma Majorca to recharge.

Her achievements outside of work include completing the UK Ironman Triathlon in 2006 and representing GB as an age group duathlon athlete in France in 2012. After retiring from triathlons in 2014, Sandra replaced them with the equally demanding pursuit of Mysore Ashtanga Yoga, which she practises six days a week in the early hours of the morning. Sandra has studied with renowned Ashtanga yoga teachers in India, Milan, Madrid, Palma and London. In addition, she still runs for pleasure twice a week, practices Transcendental Meditation and has recently started growing vegetables as the next challenge!

This is Sandra's second book. Her first book, *Own It – Regain Control and Live Life on Your Terms*, was published in 2016 by Rethink Press and is available on Amazon.

Contact

Sandra is a fully qualified professional coach and a member of the International Coach Federation and the Association of Coaching.

You can find out more about Sandra, including how to work with her, at:

- 🌐 www.sandrawebbercoaching.com
- 🌐 www.thekudosgroup.com
- 💼 www.linkedin.com/in/sandra-webber-26b275
- 📘 www.facebook.com/Sandrawebbercoachprofile
- 🐦 @sandraKudos
- 📷 @sandrakudos